Glossary of
German and English
Management Terms

Taschenwörterbuch
englischer
und deutscher
Handelsausdrücke

D1719996

Glossary of German and English Management Terms

Taschenwörterbuch englischer und deutscher Handelsausdrücke

by/von

JAMES COVENEY

and/und

CHRISTINA DEGENS

LONGMAN

Longman Group Limited
Harlow and London

Associated companies, branches and
representatives throughout the world

© Longman Group Ltd 1977

First published 1977

ISBN 0 582 55525 6

Printed in Hong Kong by
Sheck Wah Tong Printing Press

Introduction

This glossary is an attempt to fill a gap that clearly exists: the rapid growth of the management sciences in the last two decades has resulted in the coining of many new terms to describe new techniques and concepts which are not found in English-German and German-English dictionaries.

The terms included have been drawn from the main areas of management interest: business policy and corporate planning, computer techniques, finance, marketing, operational research, personnel management and, to a lesser degree, production. We have tried to keep a proper balance by not overemphasizing any one area. Generally speaking, terms which can be found in standard or commercial dictionaries have been excluded.

In selecting terms for inclusion it was decided to give priority to the broader and more general concepts over the more technical and specialised terms in management. We also decided to restrict the size of the glossary, so that it could be slipped into a businessman's briefcase; since the scope of the subject is very wide, we have therefore selected only those terms in most frequent use. We are conscious of our fallibility in selecting such terms and would be grateful if users could inform us of any obvious omissions.

No doubt some users of this glossary, both in English-speaking and German-speaking countries, will criticise or disagree with the translations we have given; we should be pleased to receive proposed alternatives for inclusion in a revised edition.

This glossary would not have appeared without the aid of the editing and translating staff in the Düsseldorf office of McKinsey and Company, Inc., and we wish to thank in particular Miss Karen A. Finney. The compilation of the glossary was based on the *Glossary of French and English Management Terms* (James Coveney and Sheila J. Moore), the first in the series, work on which was made possible by a generous grant from the McKinsey Foundation for Management Research.

James Coveney
Christina Degens

Einführung

Dieses Taschenwörterbuch hat den Zweck, eine offensichtliche Lücke auszufüllen: infolge der raschen Entwicklung der Betriebsführungswissenschaften während der letzten zwei Jahrzehnte hat man nämlich viele neue Ausdrücke prägen müssen, um neue Verfahren und Begriffe zu beschreiben, die aber noch in keinen englisch-deutschen oder deutsch-englischen Wörterbüchern enthalten sind.

Die einbezogenen Ausdrücke sind den Hauptbereichen des Betriebsführungswesens entnommen worden: Geschäftspolitik und Unternehmensplanung, Computer-Verfahren, Finanz, Handelsverkehr, Unternehmungs-forschung, Personalleitung und auch, bis zu einem gewissen Grad, Produktion. Wir haben versucht, das richtige Gleichgewicht dadurch zu behalten, indem wir kein einzelnes Gebiet besonders behandelt haben. Im allgemeinen sind alle in Standard- bzw. Handelswörter-büchern enthaltenen Ausdrücke ausgeschlossen worden.

Beim Auswählen von Ausdrücken haben wir uns entschlossen, den allgemeinen Begriffen den Vorrang vor den mehr technischen und spezialisierten Ausdrücken zu geben. Weiter haben wir uns entschlossen, die Größe des Wörterbuchs einzuschränken, so daß es leicht in die Aktentasche eines Geschäftsmannes geht: da der Umfang des Fachgebiets sehr groß ist, haben wir nur die gebräuch-lichsten Ausdrücke gewählt. Wir sind uns aber unserer Fehlbarkeit beim Auswählen solcher Ausdrücke völlig bewußt und wären den Benutzern dankbar, wenn sie uns von irgendwelchen offensichtlichen Fehlern unterrichten würden.

Einige Benutzer dieses Wörterbuchs, sowohl in englisch- als in deutschsprechenden Ländern, werden sicherlich die gegebenen Übersetzungen kritisieren oder sogar ablehnen, und wir würden uns freuen, Vorschläge für Alternativen zum Einbeziehen in eine verbesserte Auflage anzunehmen.

Ohne Hilfe der Schriftleitung und des Übersetzungs-personals des Düsseldorfer Büros McKinsey & Company Inc. wäre dieses Wörterbuch nicht erschienen: und unsern besonderen Dank an Fräulein Karen A. Finney. Der Zusammenstellung dieses Wörterbuchs liegt das *Glossary of French and English Management Terms* (James Coveney and Sheila J. Moore) zugrunde – das erste in der Serie und durch einen großzügigen Zuschuß vom McKinsey Foundation for Management Research ermöglicht.

James Coveney
Christina Degens

Note/Achtung

Terms marked with an asterisk do not have an exact equivalent in the other language: an approximate translation is given.

Sternchen zeichnen diejenigen Ausdrücke aus, die in der anderen Sprache keine genaue Entsprechung haben: bei solchen Fällen wird die nächste Übersetzung gegeben.

ENGLISH GERMAN

A

ADP (automatic data processing)	automatische Datenverarbeitung (f)
absenteeism	Fernbleiben (n), Abwesenheit (f), Fehlen (n) der Mitarbeiter (mpl), 'krank feiern'
absorption costing	Kostenaufteilungsverfahren (n)
abandonment	
product —	Streichung (f) eines Produktes (n), von Produkten (npl)
acceptance	
brand —	Markengeltung (f)
consumer —	Produktannahme (f) durch den Verbraucher (m)
access	
multi- —	mehrfacher Zugang (m)
random —	wahlfreier Zugriff (m)
accountability	Rechenschaftspflicht, Verantwortlichkeit (f)
accountant	
chief —	Hauptbuchhalter (m)
accounting	
— department	Buchhaltungs-, Rechnungs-abteilung (f)
— model	Buchhaltungsmodell (n), Kostenrechnungsart (f)
— period	Rechnungsabschnitt (m), Bilanzierungsperiode (f)
— ratio	Betriebskennziffer (f)
cost —	Kostenrechnung, Kalkulation (f)
management —	Betriebsrechnungswesen (n)
profit centre —	Kostenträgerrechnung (f)
responsibility —	verantwortungsbezogene Erfas-sung (f) von Kosten (pl) und Leistungen (fpl)
accounts	
consolidated —	konsolidierte Konten (npl)
group —	Sammelkonten (npl)
acquisition	Akquisition (f), Erwerb (m)
— profile	Akquisitionsprofil (n)
data —	Datenbeschaffung (f)
action plan	Aktionsplan, Durchführungs-plan (m)
activate (to)	aktivieren

activity	
— chart	Tätigkeitsdiagramm (*n*)
— sampling	Arbeitsstichproben (*fpl*)
support —	Unterstützung (*f*)
actualisation	
self —	Eigendynamik (*f*)
adaptive control	adaptive Kontrolle, Anpassungskontrolle (*f*)
added value	Mehrwert (*m*)
— tax (VAT)	Mehrwertsteuer (*f*)
administration	Verwaltung (*f*)
financial —	Finanzverwaltung (*f*)
administrative	
— control procedure(s)	administrative, verwaltungstechnische Kontrollverfahren (*npl*), Verfahren zur Verwaltungskontrolle (*f*)
— overheads	Verwaltungsgemeinkosten (*pl*)
— theory	Verwaltungstheorie (*f*)
advancement	
executive —	Förderung (*f*), Beförderung (*f*), Aufstieg (*m*) der Führungskräfte (*fpl*)
advantage	
competitive —	Wettbewerbsvorteil (*m*)
advertising	
— agent	Werbemittler (*m*)
— appropriation	bewilligter Werbeetat, Werbefonds (*m*), bewilligte Werbemittel (*npl*)
— budget	Werbebudget (*n*), Werbeetat (*m*)
— campaign	Werbekampagne (*f*)
— drive	Werbefeldzug (*m*), verstärkter Werbeeinsatz (*m*), verstärkter Einsatz der Werbemittel (*npl*)
— effectiveness	Werbewirksamkeit (*f*)
— manager	Werbeleiter (*m*)
— media	Werbeträger (*m*), Werbemittel (*npl*)
— message	Werbebotschaft (*f*)
— research	Werbeforschung (*f*)
— theme	Werbethema (*n*)
corporate —	Unternehmenswerbung (*f*)
product —	Produktwerbung (*f*)
subliminal —	unterschwellige Werbung (*f*)
advisory services	Beratungsdienste (*mpl*)
affiliate company	Beteiligung(-sgesellschaft), Tochtergesellschaft (*f*)

after-sales service	Kundendienst (*m*) nach dem Verkauf (*m*), Kundenbetreuung (*f*)
agent	
advertising —	Werbemittler (*m*)
sole —	Alleinvertreter (*m*)
agreement	
collective bargaining —	Tarifvertrag (*m*)
productivity —	Abkommen (*n*) über Produktivitätssteigerungen (*fpl*), Produktivitätsvereinbarung (*f*)
algorithm	Algorithmus (*m*)
allocation	
— of costs	Kostenumlage (*f*), Kostenzuschlag (*m*), Kostenaufschlüsselung (*f*)
— of responsibilities	Zuweisung (*f*) von Verantwortlichkeiten (*fpl*)
resource —	Allokation (*f*) der/von Ressourcen (*pl*), Zuteilung (*f*) von Hilfsmitteln (*npl*)
allowance	
depreciation —	Abschreibungsmöglichkeit (*f*), Zurückstellung (*f*) für Abschreibungen (*fpl*)
amalgamation	Vereinigung, Verschmelzung, Fusion, Zusammenlegung (*f*), Zusammenschluß (*m*)
analogue	
— computer (ac)	Analogrechner (*m*), Analog-Computer (*m*)
— representation	Analogdarstellung (*f*)
analysis	
breakeven —	Analyse (*f*) der Rentabilitätsschwelle (*f*)
competitor —	Konkurrenzanalyse (*f*)
contribution —	Analyse (*f*) des Deckungsbeitrages (*m*)
cost —	Kostenanalyse (*f*)
cost-benefit — (CBA)	Kosten-/Nutzenanalyse (*f*)
cost, volume, profit —	Kosten-/Umsatz-/Gewinnanalyse (*f*), Kosten-/Gewinn-/Volumenanalyse (*f*)
critical path — (CPA)	Analyse (*f*) des kritischen Pfades (*m*), Analyse der kritischen Ablaufstufen (*fpl*)

decision —	Entscheidungsanalyse (*f*)
depth —	Tiefenanalyse (*f*)
financial —	Finanzanalyse (*f*)
functional —	funktionale Analyse (*f*)
input-output —	Input-Output-Investitionsporte-folioanalyse, Input-Output-Analyse (*f*)
investment —	Investitionsanalyse (*f*)
job —	Stellenanalyse (*f*)
marginal —	Marginalanalyse (*f*)
media —	Mediaanalyse (*f*)
morphological —	morphologische Analyse (*f*)
needs —	Bedarfsanalyse (*f*)
network —	Netzanalyse (*f*)
part — training	Ausbildung (*f*) in Teilanalysen (*fpl*)
problem —	Problemanalyse (*f*)
product —	Produktanalyse (*f*)
profit factor —	Gewinnfaktoranalyse (*f*), Analyse der Gewinnfaktoren (*mpl*)
profitability —	Rentabilitätsanalyse (*f*)
project —	Projektanalyse (*f*)
regression —	Regressionsanalyse (*f*)
multiple — (MRA)	multiple Regressionsanalyse (*f*)
risk —	Risikoanalyse (*f*)
sales —	Umsatzanalyse, Verkaufsanalyse (*f*)
sensitivity —	Sensitivitätsanalyse (*f*)
sequential —	Folgeanalyse, sequentielle Analyse (*f*)
skills —	Fähigkeitsanalyse (*f*), Analyse der Fähigkeiten (*fpl*)
systems —	Systemanalyse (*f*)
user —	Benutzeranalyse (*f*)
value — (VA)	Wertanalyse (*f*)
variance —	Varianzanalyse (*f*)
analytical training	analytische Ausbildung (*f*), Ausbildung im analytischen Denken (*n*)
ancillary operations	Hilfsoperationen, Nebenoperationen (*fpl*)
anticipating response	antizipative Reaktion (*f*)
anticipatory response	antizipatorische Reaktion (*f*)
appeal	
sales —	Verkaufsappell (*m*)
apportionment	Verteilung, Aufteilung (*f*)

appraisal	Bewertung, Beurteilung (*f*)
capital expenditure —	Investitionsbewertung, -beurteilung (*f*)
financial —	Bewertung der Finanzmittel (*npl*), Finanzbewertung (*f*)
investment —	Investitionsbewertung (*f*)
market —	Marktbeurteilung (*f*)
performance —	Leistungsbewertung, -beurteilung (*f*)
resource —	Bewertung (*f*) von Ressourcen (*pl*)
self —	Selbsteinschätzung (*f*)
approach	
systems —	Systemverfahren, Systemvorgehen (*n*)
top management —	Vorgehen (*n*) der Unternehmensleitung (*f*)
appropriation	
advertising —	bewilligter Werbeetat, Werbefonds (*m*), bewilligte Werbemittel (*npl*)
budget —	bewilligtes Budget (*n*), bewilligter Budgetfonds (*m*), bewilligte Budgetmittel (*npl*)
marketing —	bewilligte Marketing-Mittel (*npl*)
aptitude test	Eignungstest (*m*)
arbitration	Schlichtungsverfahren, Schiedsverfahren (*n*)
area	
growth —	Wachstumsgebiet (*n*), Wachstumsbereich (*m*)
problem —	Problembereich (*m*)
product —	Produktbereich (*m*)
sales —	Absatzgebiet, Verkaufsgebiet (*n*)
trading—	Handelsgebiet, Absatzgebiet (*n*)
assembly line	Fliessband (*n*)
assessment	Bewertung, Beurteilung (*f*)
demand —	Nachfragebewertung (*f*)
project —	Projektbewertung (*f*)
risk —	Risikoeinschätzung, Risikobewertung (*f*)
asset	
— turnover	Umschlagshäufigkeit (*f*) des Kapitals (*n*)
— value	Substanzwert (*m*), Fundsvermögen (*n*)
assets	Aktiva (*pl*)

current —	Umlaufvermögen (*n*)
net —	Nettoumlaufvermögen (*n*), Nettowert (*m*) des Umlaufvermögens (*n*)
earnings on —	Vermögensertrag (*m*)
fixed —	Anlagevermögen (*n*)
intangible —	immaterielle Werte (*mpl*)
liquid —	flüssige Mittel, liquide Mittel (*npl*)
net —	Nettovermögen (*n*)
quick —	sofort einlösbare Guthaben (*npl*), kurzfristige Mittel (*npl*)
revaluation of —	Neubewertung (*f*) des (Anlage-) Vermögens (*n*)
tangible —	greifbare Vermögenswerte, materielle Werte (*mpl*)
assignment	Studie (*f*), Auftrag (*m*), Aufgabe (*f*)
job —	Zuteilung (*f*) von Aufgaben (*fpl*), Aufgabenzuteilung (*f*)
assistant	
— general manager	stellvertretender Generaldirektor (*m*)
— manager	stellvertretender Direktor, Geschäftsleiter (*m*)
— to manager	Direktionsassistent (*m*)
line —	Linienassistent (*m*)
staff —	Stabsassistent (*m*)
associate company	nahestehende Gesellschaft (*f*)
association	
trade —	'Berufsgenossenschaft (*f*), Wirtschafts-, Arbeitgeber-, Fachverband (*m*)
attitude	
— survey	Verhaltensanalyse (*f*)
user —	Verbrauchereinstellung (*f*), -verhalten (*n*)
— survey	Verbrauchererhebung (*f*), Benutzeranalyse (*f*)
audit (to)	Rechnungen (*fpl*) überprüfen, Revision (*f*) durchführen
audit	Rechnungs-, Bilanzprüfung (*f*)
internal —	Innenrevision, interne Rechnungsprüfung (*f*)
management —	Betriebsrechnungsprüfung (*f*)
manpower —	Überprüfung (*f*) des Personalbestandes (*m*)

operations —	Betriebsrevision, Betriebsprüfung (f)
auditing	
balance sheet —	Bilanzprüfung (f)
auditor	Rechnungsprüfer (m)
authorised capital	Stammkapital, Grundkapital, genehmigtes Kapital (n)
authority	
— structure	Weisungs-, Befugnis-, Autoritätsstruktur (f)
contraction of —	Beschränkung (f) der (von) Befugnisse(n) (fpl)
line —	Linienvollmacht, Linienbefugnis (f)
automatic data processing (ADP)	automatische Datenverarbeitung (f)
automation	Automation, Automatisierung (f)
average cost	durchschnittliche Kosten, Durchschnittskosten (pl)
awareness	
brand —	Markenbewußtsein (n)
cost —	Kostenbewußtsein (n)

B

balance sheet auditing	Bilanzprüfung (f)
bank	
computer —	Computer-Bank (f)
data —	Datenbank (f)
safety —	Sicherheitsbank (f)
bar chart	Balkendiagramm (n)
bargaining	
collective —	Tarifverhandlungen (fpl)
— agreement	Tarifvertrag (m)
plant —	innerbetriebliche Tarifverhandlung (f)
productivity —	Produktivitätsverhandlung (f), Lohnverhandlungen mit Produktivitätsvereinbarungen (fpl)
batch	
— control	Stapelkontrolle (f)
— processing	Stapelverarbeitung (f)
— production	Fabrikation (f) nach Losgrößen (fpl)
economic — quantity	wirtschaftliche Losgröße (f)

behaviour	
buying —	Kaufverhalten (*n*)
consumer —	Verbraucherverhalten (*n*)
organisational —	Verhalten (*n*) in der Organisation (*f*)
behavioural science	Verhaltensforschung (*f*)
benchmark	Richtzahl, Leitzahl, Kennziffer (*f*)
bid	
takeover —	Übernahmeangebot (*n*)
board	
— control	Aufsichtsratskontrolle (*f*)
— meeting	Aufsichtsratssitzung (*f*)
— of directors	Aufsichtsrat (*m*)
— room	Sitzungsraum (*m*)
executive —	Führungsgremium (*n*), Aufsichtsrat (*m*)
bonus	
— scheme	Prämien-, Bonusplan (*m*)
group —	Gruppenbonus (*m*)
premium —	ertragsbezogener Bonus (*m*)
book value	Buchwert (*m*)
booster training	zusätzliches Training (*n*), zusätzliche Schulung (*f*)
borrowing facility	Kreditaufnahmemöglichkeiten (*fpl*)
brains trust	Beratungsausschuss (*m*), Expertenrat, wissenschaftlicher Beirat (*m*)
brainstorming	spontane Ideenerzeugung (*f*), kreatives Denken (*n*)
branch office	Zweigstelle (*f*), Filiale (*f*) Niederlassung (*f*)
brand	Marke (*f*)
— acceptance	Markengeltung (*f*)
— awareness	Markenbewußtsein (*n*)
— image	Markenbild, -image (*n*)
— loyalty	Markentreue (*f*)
— manager	Markenbetreuer (*m*), Marken-Manager (*m*)
— recognition	Anerkennung (*f*) als Markenartikel (*m*) durch die Verbraucher (*mpl*)
— strategy	Markenstrategie (*f*)
breakdown	
operations —	Aufgliederung (*f*) des Stelleninhaltes (*m*)

breakeven	
— analysis	Analyse (*f*) der Rentabilitäts-schwelle (*f*)
— point	Kosten-, Ertrags-, Gewinn-, Rentabilitätsschwelle (*f*)
breakthrough	Durchbruch (*m*)
break-up value	Altmaterial-, Ausschlachtungs-wert (*m*)
briefing	Einweisung, Unterrichtung (*f*)
broker	Makler (*m*)
software —	Zwischenhändler (*m*) für Software-Vertrieb (*m*)
budget	
— appropriation	bewilligtes Budget (*n*), bewilligter Budgetfonds (*m*), bewilligte Budgetmittel (*npl*)
— constraint	Budgetbeschränkung (*f*)
—forecasting	Budgetprognose (*f*)
— standard(s)	Budgetnorm(en) (*f*(*pl*))
advertising —	Werbebudget (*n*). Werbeetat (*m*)
capital —	Kapitalbudget (*n*)
cash —	Kassenbudget (*n*)
flexible —	elastisches Budget (*n*)
investment —	Investitionsbudget (*n*)
marketing —	Marketing-Budget (*n*)
sales —	Verkaufsbudget (*n*)
budgetary control	Budgetkontrolle (*f*)
budgeting	Budgetierung (*f*)
— control	Budgetierungskontrolle (*f*)
capital —	Kapitalbudgetierung (*f*)
cash —	Kassenbudgetierung (*f*)
output —	Budgetierung (*f*) im Produk-tionsbereich (*m*), Output-In-vestitionsportefolio (*n*)
performance—	Leistungsplanung (*f*)
planning-program-ming- — system (PPBS)	Planungs-, Programmierungs-(und) Budgetierungssystem (*n*)
programme —	Aufstellung (*f*) des Ist-Budgets (*n*), Programmbudgetierung (*f*)
buffer stock	Sicherheitsbevorratung (*f*)
business	
— cycle	Konjunkturzyklus (*m*)
— economist	Betriebsökonom (*m*), Betriebs-wirt(-schaftler) (*m*)

— forecasting	Geschäftsprognose (*f*), Konjunkturaussage (*f*)
— game	Unternehmensspiel (*n*)
— management	Betriebsführung (*f*), Betriebswirtschaft (*f*)
— policy	Geschäftspolitik (*f*)
— relations	Geschäftsbeziehungen (*fpl*)
— strategy	Geschäftsstrategie (*f*)
buyer	
chief —	Haupteinkäufer (*m*)
potential —	potentieller Käufer (*m*)
buyers' market	Käufermarkt (*m*)
buying behaviour	Kaufverhalten (*n*)
by-product	Nebenprodukt (*n*)
— testing	Testen (*n*) des Nebenproduktes

C

CBA (cost-benefit analysis)	Kosten-/Nutzenanalyse (*f*)
COINS (computerised information system)	Informationssystem (*n*) auf Computer-Basis (*f*)
CPA (critical path analysis)	Analyse (*f*) des kritischen Pfades (*m*), Analyse der kritischen Ablaufstufen (*fpl*)
CPM (critical path method)	Methode (*f*) des kritischen Pfades (*m*)
CWM (clerical work measurement)	Leistungsbewertung (*f*) des Büropersonals (*n*), Leistungsbeurteilung (*f*) der Büroangestellten (*pl*)
campaign	
advertising —	Werbekampagne (*f*)
productivity —	Produktivitätskampagne (*f*)
canvass (to)	werben um
capacity	
— utilisation	Kapazitätsauslastung (*f*)
excess —	überschüssige Kapazität (*f*)
manufacturing —	Produktionskapazität, Fertigungskapazität (*f*)
plant —	Betriebs-Anlagenkapazität (*f*)
capital	
— budget	Kapitalbudget (*n*)
— budgeting	Kapitalbudgetierung (*f*)
— commitment	Kapitalbindung (*f*)
— employed	eingesetztes Kapital (*n*)
return on — (ROCE)	Rendite (*f*) des eingesetzten Kapitals (*n*)

— expenditure appraisal	Investitionsbewertung, -beurteilung (*f*)
— formation	Vermögensbildung, Kapitalbildung (*f*)
— goods	Investitionsgüter (*npl*)
— intensive	kapitalintensiv
— output ratio	Input-Output-Verhältnis des Investitionsportefolios (*n*), Kapital-/Produktionsrelation (*f*), -verhältnis (*n*)
— project evaluation	Bewertung (*f*) der Investitionsplanung (*f*)
— raising	Kapitalbeschaffung (*f*)
— rationing	Kapitalzuteilung (*f*)
— structure	Kapitalstruktur (*f*)
authorised —	Stamm-, Grund-, genehmigtes Kapital (*n*)
circulating —	Betriebskapital (*n*)
issued —	Emissions-, ausgegebenes Kapital (*n*)
loan —	Anleihekapital (*n*)
return on—	Kapitalrendite (*f*)
risk —	Risikokapital (*n*)
share —	Aktienkapital (*n*)
venture —	Risikokapital (*n*)
working —	Betriebskapital (*n*)
capitalisation	Kapitalisierung (*f*)
capitalise (to)	kapitalisieren, mit Kapital ausstatten
capitalised	
overcapitalised	überkapitalisiert
undercapitalised	unterkapitalisiert
career planning	Karriereplanung (*f*)
cartel	Kartell (*n*)
case study	Fallstudie (*f*)
cash	
— budget	Kassenbudget (*n*)
— budgeting	Kassenbudgetierung (*f*)
— flow	Cash Flow (*m*)
discounted — (DCF)	diskontierter Cash Flow (*m*)
incremental —	Zuwachs (*m*), Differential (*n*) des Cash Flow
— management	Verwaltung (*f*) der liquiden Mittel (*npl*)
— ratio	Kassenkennziffer (*f*)
centralisation	Zentralisierung (*f*)

centre	
computer —	Rechenzentrum (*n*)
cost —	Kostenstelle (*f*)
profit —	Gewinnzentrum (*n*), Kostenträger (*m*)
— accounting	Kostenträgerrechnung (*f*)
chain	
— of command	Instanzenzug (*m*), Führungsstruktur (*f*)
— of distribution	Vertriebskette (*f*)
chairman (if also an executive)	Vorsitzender (*m*)
deputy —	stellvertretender Vorsitzender (*m*)
vice —	stellvertretender Vorsitzender (*m*)
challenge	
job —	Stellenanforderung (*f*), Herausforderung (*f*) durch die Stelle (*f*)
change	
organisational —	organisatorische Änderung (*f*)
channels	
— of communication	Kommunikationswege (*mpl*)
— of distribution	Vertriebs-, Absatzwege (*mpl*)
chart	
activity —	Tätigkeitsdiagramm (*n*)
bar —	Balkendiagramm (*n*)
flow —	Ablaufdiagramm (*n*)
flow process —	Arbeitsablaufbogen (*m*)
management —	Organogramm (*n*) der Unternehmensführung (*f*), der Unternehmensleitung (*f*)
organisation —	Organogramm (*n*), Organisationsplan (*m*)
pie —	Kreisdiagramm (*n*)
Z- —	Z-Diagramm (*n*)
chief	
— accountant	Hauptbuchhalter (*m*)
— buyer	Haupteinkäufer (*m*)
— executive	Vorstandsvorsitzender (*m*), oberstes Führungsorgan (*n*), Generaldirektor (*m*)
circulating capital	Betriebskapital (*n*)
classification	
job —	Stellenklassifizierung (*f*)
clerical work measurement (CWM)	Leistungsbewertung (*f*) des Büropersonals (*n*), Leistungsbeurteilung (*f*) der Büroangestellten (*pl*)
closed loop	Rückkoppelungssystem (*n*)

closed shop	gewerkschaftspflichtiger Betrieb (*m*)
closing down costs	Stillegungskosten (*pl*)
collective bargaining	Tarifverhandlungen (*fpl*)
— agreement	Tarifvertrag (*m*)
collusion	Geheimabsprache (*f*)
command	
chain of —	Führungsstruktur (*f*), Instanzenzug (*m*)
line of —	Führungsstruktur (*f*), Instanzenzug (*m*), Weisungsstruktur (*f*)
commitment	
capital —	Kapitalbindung (*f*)
common language	gemeinsame Sprache (*f*), Standardcode, einheitlicher Code (*m*)
communication	
— s network	Kommunikationsnetz (*n*)
— theory	Kommunikationstheorie (*f*)
channels of —	Kommunikationswege (*mpl*)
company	
— goal	Unternehmensziel (*n*)
— objectives	Unternehmensziele (*npl*)
overall —	gesamte Unternehmensziele (*npl*), Gesamtziele (*npl*) des Unternehmens (*n*)
— philosophy	Unternehmensphilosophie (*f*)
— planning	Unternehmensplanung (*f*)
— policy	Unternehmenspolitik (*f*)
— profile	Unternehmensprofil (*n*)
— reconstruction	Wiederaufbau (*m*), Sanierung (*f*) des Unternehmens (*n*)
affiliate —	Beteiligung (*f*), Beteiligungsgesellschaft, Tochtergesellschaft (*f*)
associate —	nahestehende Gesellschaft (*f*)
holding —	Dachgesellschaft, Holdinggesellschaft (*f*)
joint venture —	Gemeinschaftsunternehmen (*n*), an einem Gemeinschaftsunternehmen beteiligte Gesellschaft (*f*)
parent —	Muttergesellschaft (*f*)
subsidiary —	Niederlassung (*f*), Tochtergesellschaft (*f*)
system managed —	nach System geführtes Unternehmen (*n*)

comparison
  interfirm —   Betriebsvergleich (*m*)
compensation
  executive —   Vergütung (*f*) der Führungs-
                              kräfte (*fpl*)

competence
  executive —   Führungsfähigkeiten (*fpl*)
  job —   Stellenqualifikationen (*fpl*)
competitive
  — advantage   Wettbewerbsvorteil (*m*)
  — edge   Wettbewerbsvorsprung (*m*)
  — position   Wettbewerbsstellung (*f*),
                              -position (*f*)
  — price   Konkurrenzpreis, konkur-
                              renzfähiger Preis (*m*)
  — stimulus   Wettbewerbsanreiz (*m*)
  — strategy   Wettbewerbsstrategie (*f*)
  — tactics   Wettbewerbstaktik (*f*)
  — thrust   Wettbewerbsvorstoß (*m*)
competitor analysis   Konkurrenzanalyse (*f*)
complex
  production —   gesamte Produktionsanlagen
                              (*fpl*)
comptroller   Rechnungs-, Bilanzprüfer (m),
                              Revisor, Controller (*m*)
computer   Computer (*m*)
  — bank   Computer-Bank (*f*)
  — centre   Rechenzentrum (*n*)
  — input   Computer-Eingabe (*f*)
  — language   Computer-Sprache, Ma-
                             schinensprache (*f*)
  — output   Computer-Ausgabe (*f*)
  — programming   Programmierung (*f*) (des
                             Computers (*m*))
  — services   Computer-Dienste (*mpl*)
    — bureau   Computer-(Dienst-)Zentrale (*f*)
  — simulation   Computer-Simulation (*f*)
  — storage   Speicherung (*f*) auf/im Com-
                             puter (*m*)
  analogue —   Analogrechner (*m*),
                             Analog-Computer (*m*)
  digital —   Digitalrechner (*m*),
                             Digital-Computer (*m*)
computerise (FO)   auf Computer (*m*) umstellen
computerised inform-   Informationssystem (*n*) auf
  ation system (COINS)   Computer-Basis (*f*)
concept
  value —   Wertkonzept (*n*)

14

conception	
product —	Produktkonzeption (f)
conciliation	Schlichtung (f)
conditions of employment	Arbeitsbedingungen (fpl)
conglomerate	Konglomerat (n)
consciousness	
cost —	Kostenbewußtsein (n)
consolidated accounts	konsolidierte Konten (npl)
consolidation	Konsolidierung (f)
consortium	Konsortium (n), Gruppe (f)
constraint	
budget —	Budgetbeschränkung (f)
consultancy	Beratungsunternehmen (n)
consultant	
(management —)	Unternehmensberater (m)
consultation	
joint —	gemeinsame Beratung (f)
consumer	
— acceptance	Produktannahme (f) durch den Verbraucher (m)
— behaviour	Verbraucherverhalten (n)
— goods	Verbrauchs-, Konsumgüter (npl)
— research	Verbraucherforschung (f)
— resistance	Produktablehnung (f) durch den Verbraucher (m)
— satisfaction	Befriedigung (f) der Konsumentenwünsche (mpl), Befriedigung (f) der Nachfrage (f)
consumers' panel	Verbraucherpanel (n)
containerisation	Umstellung (f) auf Container (m)
content	
work —	Stelleninhalt, Arbeitsinhalt (m)
contingency reserve	Eventualrückstellungen (fpl), Rücklage (f) für unvorhergesehene Risiken (npl)
continuous	
— flow production	fortlaufender Produktionsablauf (m), Massenproduktion (f)
— stock taking	fortlaufende Lager-, Bestandsaufnahme (f), fortlaufende Lagerbestandsaufnahme (f)
contract	Vertrag (m)
work by —	Arbeit (f) gemäß vertraglicher Vereinbarung (f)
contraction of authority	Beschränkung (f) der (von) Befugnisse(n) (fpl)

15

control	Kontrolle (*f*)
— information	Kontrollinformation (*f*)
adaptive —	adaptive Kontrolle, Anpassungs-kontrolle (*f*)
administrative — procedure	administrative, verwaltungstech-nische Kontrollverfahren (*npl*), Verfahren (*n*) zur Verwaltungs-kontrolle (*f*)
batch —	Stapelkontrolle (*f*)
board —	Aufsichtsratskontrolle (*f*)
budgetary/ budgeting —	Budgetkontrolle, Budgetierungs-kontrolle (*f*)
cost —	Kostenkontrolle (*f*)
credit —	Kreditkontrolle (*f*)
financial —	Finanzkontrolle (*f*)
inventory —	Lagerbestandskontrolle (*f*)
managerial —	Kontrolle (*f*) durch Unter-nehmensleitung (*f*), Führungs-kontrolle (*f*)
manufacturing —	Fertigungs-, Produktions-kontrolle (*f*)
numerical —	numerische Kontrolle (*f*)
process —	Verfahrens-, Fertigungskontrolle (*f*)
production —	Produktionskontrolle (*f*)
production planning and —	Produktionsplanung und -kontrolle (*f*)
progress —	Fortschrittskontrolle (*f*)
quality — (QC)	Qualitätskontrolle (*f*)
total —	umfassende Qualitätskontrolle (*f*)
span of —	Kontrollspanne (*f*)
statistical —	statistische Kontrolle (*f*)
stock —	Lagerbestandskontrolle (*f*)
controller	Controller, Bilanz-, Rechnungs-prüfer (*m*)
corporate	
— advertising	Unternehmenswerbung (*f*)
— growth	Unternehmenswachstum (*n*)
— image	Unternehmensimage (*n*)
— model	Unternehmensmodell (*n*)
— planning	Unternehmensplanung (*f*)
— strategy	Unternehmensstrategie (*f*)
— structure	Unternehmensstruktur (*f*)
corporation tax	Körperschaftssteuer (*f*)
cost	
— accounting	Kostenrechnung, Kalkulation (*f*
— analysis	Kostenanalyse (*f*)

— awareness	Kostenbewußtsein (*n*)
— benefit analysis (CBA)	Kosten-/Nutzenanalyse (*f*)
— centre	Kostenstelle (*f*)
— consciousness	Kostenbewußtsein (*n*)
— control	Kostenkontrolle (*f*)
— effectiveness	Kostenwirksamkeit (*f*)
— factor	Kostenfaktor (*m*)
— of production	Produktionskosten (*pl*)
— reduction	Kostensenkung, Rationalisierung (*f*)
— standard	Kalkulationsnorm (*f*)
— structure	Kostenstruktur (*f*)
— variance	Kostenabweichung (*f*)
—, volume, profit analysis	Kosten-/Gewinn-/Volumenanalyse, Kosten-/Umsatz-/Gewinnanalyse (*f*)
average —	Durchschnitts-, durchschnittliche Kosten (*pl*)
closing-down —	Stillegungskosten (*pl*)
direct —	direkte Kosten (*pl*)
indirect —	indirekte Kosten (*pl*)
marginal —	Marginalkosten, Grenzkosten (*pl*)
on- —	Regiekosten (*pl*), Kostenzuschlag (*m*), allgemeine Handlungskosten (*pl*)
opportunity —	alternative Kosten (*pl*)
replacement —	Wiederbeschaffungskosten (*pl*), -wert (*m*)
osts	
allocation of —	Kostenumlage (*f*), Kostenzuschlag (*m*), Kostenaufschlüsselung (*f*)
distribution —	Vertriebskosten (*pl*)
fixed —	fixe Kosten (*pl*)
estimating systems —	Systemkostenvoranschlag (*m*)
managed —	kontrollierte Kosten (*pl*)
production —	Produktionskosten (*pl*)
set-up —	Anlaufkosten (*pl*)
standard —	Standardkosten, Sollkosten (*pl*)
variable —	variable Kosten (*pl*)
semi- —	sprungfixe Kosten (*pl*)
osting	Kostenrechnung (*f*)
absorption —	Kostenaufteilungsverfahren (*n*)
direct —	Kostenspezifikationsverfahren (*n*), Produkt-, Grenzkostenrechnung (*f*)

council

functional —	funktionale Kostenrechnung (f
process —	Kostenrechnung (f) für Serienfertigung (f)
product —	Produktkostenrechnung (f), Ermittlung (f) der Erzeugniskosten (pl)
standard —	Standard-, Plankostenrechnung (f)
variable —	variable Kostenrechnung (f)

council

works —	Betriebsrat (m)

counselling

employee —	Personalberatung (f)
cover ratio	Deckungsverhältnis (n)

coverage

sales —	Marktabdeckung (f), Abdeckur (f) durch den Verkauf (m)

creative

— marketing	kreatives Marketing (n)
— thinking	kreatives Denken (n)

credit

— control	Kreditkontrolle (f)
— management	Kreditverwaltung (f)
— rating	Bonität (f)
self liquidating —	*ein Kredit, der sich selbst liquidiert

criteria

investment —	Investitionskriterien (npl)

critical

— mass	kritische Masse (f)
— path analysis (CPA)	Analyse (f) des kritischen Pfade (m), der kritischen Ablaufstufen (fpl)
— path method (CPM)	Methode (f) des kritischen Pfades (m)
crosslicensing	Lizenzaustausch (m)

current

— assets	Umlaufvermögen (n)
net —	Nettoumlaufvermögen (n), Nettowert (m) des Umlaufvermögens (n)
— expenditure	laufende Betriebskosten, laufende Betriebsausgaben (fpl)
— liabilities	laufende, kurzfristige Verbindlichkeiten (fpl)
— ratio	Liquiditätskennzahl (f)

curve

learning —	Lernkurve (f)

salary progression —	Gehaltsprogressionskurve (*f*)
customer	
— orientation	Kundenausrichtung (*f*)
— profile	Kundenprofil (*n*)
— service	Kundendienst (*m*)
cut prices (to)	Preise (*mpl*) senken, herabsetzen
cutting	
price —	Preisunterbietung (*f*)
cybernetics	Kybernetik (*f*)
cycle	
business —	Konjunkturzyklus (*m*)
life — (of a product)	Lebenszyklus (*m*) (eines Produktes)
work —	Arbeitszyklus (*m*)

D

DCF (discounted cash flow)	diskontierter Cash Flow (*m*)
data	
— acquisition	Datenbeschaffung (*f*)
— bank	Datenbank (*f*)
— gathering	Datensammlung (*f*)
— processing	Datenverarbeitung (*f*)
automatic — (ADP)	automatische Datenverarbeitung (*f*)
electronic — (EDP)	elektronische Datenverarbeitung (*f*)
deal	
package —	Kopplungsgeschäft (*n*)
debentures	Pfandbrief (*m*)
debt ratio	Verschuldungsgrad (*m*)
debtors	Schuldner (*mpl*)
debug (to)	überprüfen, Fehler beseitigen, testen
decentralisation	Dezentralisierung (*f*)
decision	
— analysis	Entscheidungsanalyse (*f*)
— making	Entscheidungsfindung (*f*)
— model	Entscheidungsmodell (*n*)
— process	Entscheidungsprozess (*m*)
— theory	Entscheidungstheorie (*f*)
— tree	Entscheidungsbaum (*m*)
make or buy —	Wahl (*f*) zwischen Eigenfertigung (*f*) und Kauf (*m*)
defensive strategy	defensive Strategie (*f*)
delegation	Delegation (*f*)

demand assessment	Nachfragebewertung (*f*)
democracy	
industrial —	Mitbestimmung (*f*)
department	
accounting —	Rechnungs-, Buchhaltungsabteilung (*f*)
engineering and design —	technische Abteilung (*f*) und Konstruktionsbüro (*n*)
personnel —	Personalabteilung (*f*)
planning —	Planungsabteilung (*f*)
research —	Forschungsabteilung (*f*)
sales —	Verkaufsabteilung (*f*)
departmental planning	Abteilungsplanung (*f*)
departmentalisation	Dezentralisation (*f*), betriebliche Aufgliederung (*f*)
deployment	Einsatz (*m*), Entfaltung (*f*)
depreciation allowance	Abschreibungsmöglichkeit (*f*), Zurückstellung (*f*) für Abschreibungen (*fpl*)
depth	
— analysis	Tiefenanalyse (*f*)
— interview	Tiefeninterview (*n*)
deputy	
— chairman	stellvertretender Vorsitzender (*m*)
— manager	stellvertretender Direktor, Manager (*m*)
— managing director	stellvertretender Generaldirektor (*m*)
description	
job —	Stellenbeschreibung (*f*)
design	
— engineering	Konstruktion (*f*), Konstruktionstechnik (*f*)
engineering and — department	technische Abteilung (*f*) und Konstruktionsbüro (*n*)
job —	Stellenentwurf (*m*)
product —	Produktgestaltung (*f*)
systems —	Systementwicklung, -gestaltung (*f*)
desk research	Schreibtischforschung (*f*)
determination	
price —	Preisfestsetzung (*f*)
development	
— potential	Entwicklungspotential (*n*)
— programme	Entwicklungsprogramm (*n*)
management, executive —	Führungskräfteentwicklung (*f*), Entwicklung (*f*) der Führungskräfte (*fpl*)

organisational —	Aufbau (*m*), Entwicklung (*f*) der Organisation (*f*), organisatorische Entwicklung (*f*)
product —	Produktentwicklung (*f*)
new —	Entwicklung (*f*) neuer Produkte (*npl*)
research and — (R & D)	Forschung und Entwicklung (*f*)
deviation	
standard —	Standardabweichung, Normalabweichung (*f*)
diagnostic routine	Beseitigung (*f*) von Fehlerquellen (*fpl*)
diagram	
scatter —	Punkte-, Streudiagramm, Streubild (*n*)
differential	
price —	Preisunterschied (*m*), Preisgefälle (*n*)
wage —	Lohngefälle (*n*)
differentiation	
product —	Produktdifferenzierung (*f*)
digital computer	Digitalrechner, Digital-Computer (*m*)
dilution	
— of equity	Wertverschlechterung (*f*) durch Grundstückbelastung (*f*)
— of labour	Einstellung (*f*) ungelernter Arbeitskräfte (*fpl*)
direct	
— cost	direkte Kosten (*pl*)
— costing	Produktkosten-, Grenzkostenrechnung (*f*), Kostenspezifikationsverfahren (*n*)
— expenses	direkte Ausgaben (*fpl*)
— labour	Fertigungslohn, Fabrikationslohn (*m*), unmittelbar geleistete Arbeitszeit (*f*)
— mail	Postversandwerbung (*f*)
— selling	Direktverkauf (*m*)
director	Direktor (*m*)
board of —s	Aufsichtsrat (*m*)
executive —	geschäftsführender Direktor, Generaldirektor (*m*)
non- —	nicht geschäftsführender Direktor (*m*)
financial —	Finanzdirektor (*m*)

21

managing —	Generaldirektor (*m*)
deputy —	stellvertretender General- direktor (*m*)
outside —	*dem Unternehmen (*n*) nicht unmittelbar zugehöriger Direktor (*m*)
directorate	
interlocking —	Schachtelaufsichtsrat (*m*)
discounted cash flow (DCF)	diskontierter Cash Flow (*m*)
discretion	
time span of —	zulässige Zeitspanne (*f*), zulässiger Zeitraum (*m*) für unterdurchschnittliche Leistung (*f*)
diseconomy of scale	Kostenprogression (*f*)
disincentive	fehlender, negativer Anreiz (*m*)
disinvestment	Desinvestition (*f*)
dispatching	Abfertigung (*f*)
disposition	
source and — of funds	Mittelherkunft (*f*) und -einsatz (*m*)
dispute	
labour —	Arbeitskonflikt (*m*)
dissolution	Auflösung, Liquidation (*f*)
distribution	
— costs	Vertriebskosten (*pl*)
— manager	Vertriebsleiter (*m*)
— network	Vertriebsnetz (*n*)
— planning	Vertriebsplanung (*f*)
— policy	Vertriebspolitik (*f*)
chain of —	Vertriebskette (*f*)
channels of —	Vertriebswege, Absatzwege (*mpl*)
frequency —	Häufigkeitsverteilung (*f*)
physical —	innerbetriebliche Warenverteil-
management	ung (*f*)
diversification	Diversifikation (*f*)
— strategy	Diversifikationsstrategie (*f*)
product —	Produktdiversifizierung (*f*), Produktionsbreite (*f*)
diversify (to)	diversifizieren
divestment	Besitzentziehung (*f*)
dividends	Dividenden (*fpl*)
— policy	Dividendenpolitik (*f*)
division	
operating —	Betriebsabteilung (*f*), operative Sparte (*f*)

divisional management	Spartenleitung (*f*)
double taxation relief	Steuererleichterung (*f*) bei Doppelbesteuerung (*f*)
down the line	auf nachgeordneten Führungsebenen (*fpl*)
down time	Ausfallzeit (*f*)
drive	
advertising —	Wettbewerbsfeldzug (*m*), verstärkter Einsatz (*m*) der Werbemittel (*npl*), verstärkter Werbeeinsatz (*m*)
productivity —	Produktivitätskampagne (*f*), gezielte Bemühungen (*fpl*) um Produktivitätssteigerung (*f*)
sales —	Verkaufskampagne (*f*)
dumping	Dumping (*n*)
dynamic	
— evaluation	dynamische Bewertung (*f*)
— management model	dynamisches Führungsmodell (*n*), dynamisches Management-Modell (*n*)
— programming	dynamische Programmierung (*f*)
dynamics	
group —	Gruppendynamik (*f*)
industrial —	Industriedynamik, Betriebsdynamik (*f*)
market —	Marktdynamik (*f*)
product —	Produktdynamik (*f*)

E

EDP (electronic data processing)	elektronische Datenverarbeitung (*f*)
earning	
— power	Ertragskraft (*f*)
earnings	
— on assets	Vermögensertrag (*m*)
— per share	Gewinn (*m*) pro Aktie (*f*), Ertrag (*m*) pro Aktie (*f*)
— performance	Ertragsleistung (*f*)
— yield	Erlöse (*mpl*)
price- — ratio (P/E)	Aktienpreis (*m*)/Ertragsrelation (*f*), -verhältnis (*n*)
retained —	einbehaltener Gewinn, thesaurierter Gewinn (*m*)
economic	
— batch quantity	wirtschaftliche Losgrösse (*f*)
— intelligence	Wirtschaftsinformation (*f*)

— life	Wirtschaftsleben (*n*)
— manufacturing quantity	wirtschaftliche Produktionsmenge (*f*)
— mission	wirtschaftlicher Auftrag (*m*)
— order quantity	wirtschaftliche Losgröße (*f*)
— research	Wirtschaftsforschung (*f*)
— trend	Konjunkturtrend (*m*), Konjunkturverlauf (*m*), Wirtschaftstendenzen (*fpl*)
economist	
business —	Betriebswirt, Betriebsökonom (*m*)
economy	
— of scale	Kostendegression (*f*)
motion —	Bewegungsökonomie (*f*)
edge	
competitive —	Wettbewerbsvorsprung (*m*)
effective management	wirksame Unternehmensführung (*f*), -leitung (*f*)
effectiveness	Wirksamkeit (*f*)
advertising —	Werbewirksamkeit (*f*)
cost —	Kostenwirksamkeit (*f*)
managerial —	wirksame Unternehmensführung (*f*), -leitung (*f*)
organisational —	organisatorische Wirksamkeit (*f*)
efficiency	Leistungsfähigkeit, Effizienz (*f*)
effort	
sales expansion —	Bemühungen (*fpl*) um Verkaufssteigerungen (*fpl*)
elasticity	Elastizität (*f*)
electronic data processing (EDP)	elektronische Datenverarbeitung (*f*)
employed	
capital —	eingesetztes Kapital (*n*)
return on — (ROCE)	Rendite (*f*) des eingesetzten Kapitals (*n*)
employee	
— counselling	Personalberatung (*f*)
— relations	Beziehungen (*fpl*) zu Arbeitnehmern (*mpl*)
employment	
conditions of —	Arbeitsbedingungen (*fpl*)
engineering	
— and design department	technische Abteilung (*f*) und Konstruktionsbüro (*n*)
design —	Konstruktion (*f*), Konstruktionstechnik (*f*)
human —	experimentelle Anwendung (*f*)

	psychologischer Erkenntnisse (*fpl*) auf menschliche Probleme (*npl*) im Betrieb (*m*)
industrial —	Betriebsstudie (*f*), industrielle Fertigungstechnik (*f*)
methods —	Methodentechnik (*f*), Methodik (*f*)
production —	Produktionstechnik (*f*)
systems —	Systemtechnik (*f*)
value —	Werttechnik (*f*)
enlargement	
job —	Stellenerweiterung (*f*)
enrichment	
job —	Bereicherung (*f*) durch die Stelle
entrepreneurial spirit	unternehmerische Einstellung (*f*)
environment	Umwelt (*f*)
environmental forecasting	Wirtschaftsprognose (*f*)
equipment	
— leasing	Maschinenmiete (*f*)
peripheral —	Peripheriegeräte (*npl*)
process — layout	Betriebsanlage (*f*) nach Werkstattprinzip (*n*)
equity	Eigenkapital (*n*)
dilution of —	Wertverschlechterung (*f*) durch Grundstückbelastung (*f*)
return on —	Rendite (*f*) des Eigenkapitals (*n*)
ergonometrics	Ergonometrik (*f*)
ergonomics	Ergonomik (*f*)
escalation	
price —	sich gegenseitig verstärkender Preisauftrieb (*m*)
espionage	
industrial —	Industriespionage (*f*)
estimate	
sales —	Umsatz-, Verkaufsschätzung (*f*)
estimating systems costs	Systemkostenvoranschlag (*m*)
evaluation	
capital project —	Bewertung (*f*) der Investitionsplanung (*f*)
dynamic —	dynamische Bewertung (*f*)
job —	Stellenbewertung (*f*), -beurteilung (*f*)
performance —	Leistungsbewertung (*f*)
exception	
management by —	Management by exception, Eingreifen (*n*) nur bei Abweichungen (*fpl*)

excess capacity	überschüssige Kapazität (*f*)
execution	
policy —	Durchführung (*f*) der Unternehmenspolitik (*f*)
executive	Führungskraft (*f*)
— advancement	(Be-) Förderung (*f*), Aufstieg (*m*) der Führungskräfte (*fpl*)
— board	Aufsichtsrat (*m*), Führungsgremium (*n*)
— compensation	Vergütung (*f*) der Führungskräfte (*fpl*)
— competence	Führungsfähigkeit (*f*)
— development	Führungskräfteentwicklung (*f*), Entwicklung der Führungskräfte (*fpl*)
— director	Generaldirektor (*m*), geschäftsführender Direktor (*m*)
— manpower strategy	Führungskräftestrategie (*f*)
— search	(An-) Werbung (*f*), Vermittlung (*f*) von Führungskräften (*fpl*)
chief —	Generaldirektor, Vorstandsvorsitzender (*m*), oberstes Führungsorgan (*n*)
line —	Linienführungskraft (*f*)
expansion	
— strategy	Wachstums-, Expansionsstrategie (*f*)
sales — effort	Bemühungen (*fpl*) um Verkaufssteigerungen (*fpl*)
expectations	
job —	mit einer Stelle (*f*) verbundene Erwartungen (*fpl*)
sales —	Umsatz-, Verkaufserwartungen (*fpl*)
expenditure	
current —	laufende Betriebsausgaben (*fpl*), -kosten (*pl*)
expenses	
direct —	direkte Ausgaben (*fpl*)
indirect —	indirekte Ausgaben (*fpl*)
recovery of —	Aufteilungsverfahren (*n*) für indirekte Kosten (*pl*)
running —	laufende Ausgaben (*fpl*)
exploration	
market —	Markterkundung (*f*)
exponential	
— smoothing	Exponentialausgleichung (*f*)
— trends	exponentieller Trend (*m*)

extension services	Fortbildungsangebote (*npl*)
external relations	Aussenbeziehungen (*fpl*)

F

factor	Faktor (*m*)
cost —	Kostenfaktor (*m*)
load —	Auslastungsfaktor (*m*)
profit — analysis	Analyse (*f*) der Gewinnfaktoren (*mpl*), Gewinnfaktoranalyse (*f*)
factoring	Ankauf (*m*) offener Buchforderungen (*fpl*), Debitorenverkauf (*m*)
factory overheads	Fabrikgemeinkosten (*pl*)
family tree	Stammbaum (*m*)
feasibility study	Durchführbarkeitsstudie (*f*)
feather bedding	Einstellung (*f*) nicht benötigter Arbeitskräfte (*fpl*)
feedback	Rückkoppelung (*f*)
field	
— research	Primärerhebung (*f*)
— testing	Überprüfung (*f*) im Feld (*n*), Feld-Tests (*mpl*)
financial	
— administration	Finanzverwaltung (*f*)
— analysis	Finanzanalyse (*f*)
— appraisal	Bewertung (*f*) der Finanzmittel (*npl*), Finanzbewertung (*f*)
— control	Finanzkontrolle (*f*)
— director	Finanzdirektor (*m*)
— management	Finanzverwaltung (*f*)
— planning	Finanzplanung (*f*)
— ratio	Finanzkennziffer (*f*)
— review	Finanzüberprüfung (*f*), Überprüfung (*f*) der Finanzlage (*f*)
— standards	Finanznormen (*fpl*)
— strategy	Finanzstrategie (*f*)
— year	Finanz-, Geschäfts-, Rechnungsjahr (*n*)
financing	
self —	Selbstfinanzierung, Eigenfinanzierung (*f*)
first-line manager	Führungskraft (*f*) der untersten (Führungs- Ebene (*f*))
fiscal year	Geschäfts-, Rechnungs-, Wirtschaftsjahr (*n*)
fixed	
— assets	Anlagevermögen (*n*)

fixing

— cost	fixe Kosten (*pl*)

fixing

price —	Preisfestsetzung (*f*)
flexible budget	elastisches Budget (*n*)
flotation	in Umlauf (*m*) setzen, Emission (*f*)

flow

— chart	Ablaufdiagramm (*n*)
— line	Produktionsfluß (*m*)
— process chart	Arbeitsablaufbogen (*m*)
— production	Massenproduktion (*f*)
continuous —	fortlaufender Produktionsablauf (*m*)
cash —	Cash Flow (*m*)
discounted — (DCF)	diskontierter Cash Flow (*m*)
incremental —	Zuwachs (*m*), Differential (*n*) des Cash Flow (*n*)
fund —s	Kapitalströme (*mpl*)
information —s	Informationsfluß (*m*)
follow-up	Nachfassen (*n*), Überprüfung (*f*) nach der Ausführung (*f*)

force

market —s	Marktkräfte (*fpl*)
sales —	Aussendienst (*m*)
task —	Arbeitsgruppe (*f*), Arbeitsgemeinschaft (*f*)

forecast

	Prognose (*f*)
market —	Marktprognose (*f*)
sales —	Umsatzprognose (*f*)
technological —	Prognose der technologischen Entwicklung (*f*)

forecasting

budget —	Budgetprognose (*f*)
business —	Geschäftsprognose, Konjunkturvoraussage (*f*)
environmental —	Wirtschaftsprognose (*f*)
manpower —	Prognose (*f*) des Personalbedarfes (*m*)
foreman	Vorarbeiter, Meister (*m*)

formation

capital —	Vermögensbildung, Kapitalbildung (*f*)

formulation

policy —	Formulierung der Unternehmenspolitik (*f*)
strategy —	Formulierung der Unternehmensstrategie (*f*)

28

forward planning	Vorwärtsplanung (*f*)
frequency distribution	Häufigkeitsverteilung (*f*)
fringe	
— benefit	Sozialleistungen (*fpl*), Vergütung (*f*) neben Gehalt (*n*) oder Lohn (*m*)
— market	Randmarkt (*m*)
function	Funktion (*f*)
managerial —	Führungsfunktion (*f*)
functional	
— analysis	funktionale Analyse (*f*)
— costing	funktionale Kostenrechnung (*f*)
— layout	funktionale Aufteilung (*f*)
— management	funktionales Management (*n*)
— organisation	funktionale Organisation (*f*)
— relations	funktionale Beziehungen (*fpl*)
— responsibility	funktionale Verantwortlichkeiten (*fpl*)
fund	
sinking —	Amortisations-, Tilgungsfonds (*m*)
— flows	Kapitalströme (*mpl*)
funds	
source and disposition of —	Mittelherkunft (*f*) und -einsatz (*m*)

G

game	
— theory	Spieltheorie (*f*)
business —	Unternehmensspiel (*n*)
management —	Führungs-, Unternehmensspiel (*n*)
gathering	
data —	Datensammlung (*f*)
gap study	Analyse (*f*) der Abweichungen (*fpl*)
gearing	Kapitalausstattung (*f*)
general	
— manager	Generaldirektor (*m*)
— management	allgemeines Management (*n*)
generation	
product —	Produkterzeugung (*f*)
go public (to)	an der Börse (*f*) zugelassen werden
goal	
— seeking	Zielfindung (*f*)
— setting	Zielsetzung (*f*)

company —	Unternehmensziel (*n*)
hierarchy of —s	Zielhierarchie (*f*)
profit —	Gewinnziel (*n*)
sales —	Umsatzziel (*n*)
goods	
capital —	Investitionsgüter (*npl*)
consumer —	Konsumgüter, Verbrauchsgüter (*npl*)
industrial —	Industriegüter, Investitionsgüter (*npl*)
goodwill	Firmenwert (*m*)
go-slow	Bummelstreik (*m*)
grid	
— structure	Gitterstruktur (*f*)
managerial —	Ausbildungsmethode (*f*) für Führungskräfte (*fpl*)
grievance procedure	Beschwerdeverfahren (*n*)
gross	
— margin	Bruttomarge (*f*), Bruttogewinn (*m*)
— profit	Bruttogewinn (*m*)
group	
— accounts	Sammelkonten (*npl*)
— bonus	Gruppenbonus (*m*)
— dynamics	Gruppendynamik (*f*)
— incentive	Gruppenanreiz (*m*)
— training	Gruppenausbildung (*f*), Gruppentraining (*n*)
T- —	T-Gruppentraining (*n*)
product —	Produktgruppe (*f*)
growth	
— area	Wachstumsgebiet (*n*), -bereich (*m*)
— index	Wachstumsindex (*m*)
— industry	Wachstumsindustrie (*f*)
— potential	Wachstumspotential (*n*)
— strategy	Wachstumsstrategie (*f*)
corporate —	Unternehmenswachstum (*n*)
personal —	persönliche Weiterentwicklung (*f*)
gues(s)timate	Raten und Schätzen (*n*) aufgrund bekannter Informationen (*fpl*)
guidance	
vocational —	Berufsberatung (*f*)

H

handling	
information —	Informationsbearbeitung (*f*)

materials —	Materialwirtschaft (f), Transportwesen (n), innerbetriebliches Förderwesen (n)
hard selling	aggressive Verkaufsmethoden (fpl), aggressive Verkaufspolitik (f)
hardware	Hardware (f)
head office	Hauptbüro (n), Zentrale (f)
hedge (to)	absichern
hedging operation	Hedge-Geschäft, Sicherungsgeschäft (n)
heuristics	Heuristik (f)
hierarchy of goals	Zielhierarchie (f)
hire	
plant —	Anlagenmiete (f)
hold margins (to)	Gewinnmargen (fpl) halten
holding company	Holdinggesellschaft, Dachgesellschaft (f)
holidays	
staggered —	gestaffelter Urlaub (m)
horizontal integration	horizontale Integration (f)
human	
— engineering	experimentelle Anwendung (f) psychologischer Erkenntnisse (fpl) auf menschliche Probleme (npl) im Betrieb (m)
— relations	menschliche Beziehungen (fpl) im Betrieb (m), Betriebsklima (n)

I

IPM (integrated project management)	integriertes Projekt-Management (n)
IRR (internal rate of return)	interne Rendite (f)
image	
brand —	Markenimage (n), Markenbild (n)
corporate —	Unternehmensimage (n)
product —	Produktimage (n)
impact	Auswirkung (f)
profit —	Gewinnauswirkung (f)
implementation	
strategy —	Durchführung (f) der Strategie (f)
implication	
profit —	Gewinnauswirkung (f)

31

improvement	
job —	Stellenanhebung (*f*)
product —	Produktverbesserung (*f*)
profit —	Gewinnverbesserung (*f*)
in plant training	Training (*n*) im Betrieb (*m*), innerbetriebliches Training (*n*)
incentive	
— scheme	Anreizplan (*m*)
group —	Gruppenanreiz (*m*)
incremental cash flow	Zuwachs (*m*) des Cash Flow (*m*), Differential (*n*) des Cash Flow (*m*)
index	
growth —	Wachstumsindex (*m*)
indirect	
— cost	indirekte Kosten (*pl*)
— expenses	indirekte Ausgaben (*fpl*)
— labour	Gemeinkostenlohn, Hilfslohn (*m*)
induction	Einführung (*f*) neuer Mitarbeiter (*mpl*) in das Unternehmen (*n*)
industrial	
— democracy	Mitbestimmung (*f*)
— dynamics	Industriedynamik, Betriebsdynamik (*f*)
— engineering	Betriebsstudie (*f*), industrielle Fertigungstechnik (*f*)
— espionage	Industriespionage (*f*)
— goods	Industriegüter, Investitionsgüter (*npl*)
— psychology	Betriebspsychologie (*f*)
— relations	Beziehungen (*fpl*) der Sozialpartner (*mpl*) zueinander
— security	Betriebssicherheit (*f*)
industry	
growth —	Wachstumsindustrie (*f*)
training within — (TWI)	Ausbildung (*f*) in Betriebsmethoden (*fpl*) und Arbeitsbeziehungen (*fpl*)
informal organisation	informelle Organisation (*f*)
information	
— flow	Informationsfluß (*m*)
— handling	Informationsbearbeitung (*f*)
— network	Informationsnetz (*n*)
— processing	Informationsverarbeitung (*f*)
— retrieval	Wiedergewinnung (*f*), Archivierung (*f*) von Informationen (*fpl*)
— system	Informationssystem (*n*)

computerised — (COINS)	Informationssystem (*n*) auf Computer-Basis (*f*)
management — (MIS)	Management-Informations-system (*n*)
— technology	Informationstechnologie (*f*)
— theory	Informationstheorie (*f*)
control —	Kontrollinformation(en) (*f(pl)*)
management —	Management-Information(en) (*f(pl)*)
— system (MIS)	Management-Informations-system (*n*)
input	Eingabe (*f*)
— -output analysis	Input-Output-Analyse (*f*), Input-Output-Investitionsporte-folioanalyse (*f*)
— -output table	Input-Output-Tabelle (*f*), Input-Output-Investitionsporte-foliotabelle (*f*)
computer —	Computer-Eingabe (*f*)
inspection	
staff —	Überprüfung (*f*), Untersuchung (*f*) des Personals (*n*)
intangible assets	immaterielle Werte (*mpl*)
integrated	
— management system	intergriertes Management-System (*n*)
— project manage-ment (IPM)	integriertes Projekt-Management (*n*)
integration	
horizontal —	horizontale Integration (*f*)
vertical —	vertikale Integration (*f*)
intelligence	
economic —	Wirtschaftsinformation (*f*)
market —	Marktinformationen (*fpl*)
intensive	
— production	intensive Produktion (*f*)
capital —	kapitalintensiv
labour —	arbeitsintensiv
interdependence	
strategic —	strategische Wechselbeziehung (*f*)
interest	
job —	Interesse (*n*) an der Arbeit (*f*), der Stelle (*f*)
majority —	Mehrheitsbeteiligung (*f*)
minority —	Minderheitsbeteiligung (*f*)
interface	Berührungspunkte (*mpl*), Wechselbeziehungen (*fpl*)

interfirm comparison	Betriebsvergleich (*m*)
interlocking directorate	Schachtelaufsichtsrat (*m*)
internal	
— audit	interne Rechnungsprüfung (*f*), Innenrevision (*f*)
— rate of return (IRR)	interne Rendite (*f*)
interview	
depth —	Tiefeninterview (*n*)
intuitive management	intuitive Unternehmensführung (*f*)
inventory	
— control	Lager-, Lagerbestands-, Bestandskontrolle (*f*)
— turnover	Lagerumschlag (*m*)
perpetual —	fortlaufende Lagerbestandsaufnahme (*f*)
investment	
— analysis	Investitionsanalyse (*f*)
— appraisal	Investitionsbewertung (*f*)
— budget	Investitionsbudget (*n*)
— criteria	Investitionskriterien (*npl*)
— management	Verwaltung (*f*) von Kapitalanlagen (*fpl*)
— mix	Investitionsportefeuille (*n*)
— policy	Investitionspolitik (*f*)
— programme	Investitionsprogramm (*n*)
return on —	Investitionsrentabilität (*f*), -rendite (*f*)
issued capital	Emissionskapital, ausgegebenes Kapital (*n*)

J

job	
— analysis	Stellenanalyse (*f*)
— assignment	Aufgabenzuteilung (*f*)
— challenge	Herausforderung (*f*) durch die Aufgabe (*f*), Stellenanforderung (*f*)
— classification	Stellenklassifizierung (*f*)
— competence	Stellenqualifikationen (*fpl*)
— description	Stellenbeschreibung (*f*)
— design	Stellenentwurf (*m*)
— enlargement	Stellenerweiterung (*f*)
— enrichment	Bereicherung (*f*) durch die Stelle (*f*)
— evaluation	Stellenbewertung (*f*), -beurteilung (*f*)

— expectations	mit einer Stelle (*f*) verbundene Erwartungen (*fpl*)
— improvement	Stellenanhebung (*f*)
— interest	Interesse (*n*) an der Stelle, an der Arbeit (*f*)
— performance	Leistung (*f*) in der Stelle, in einer Stelle (*f*)
— rotation	systematischer Arbeitsplatzwechsel (*m*)
— satisfaction	Befriedigung (*f*) durch die Stelle, durch die Aufgabe (*f*)
— security	sicherer Arbeitsplatz (*m*)
— simplification	Stellenvereinfachung (*f*)
— specification	Stellenanforderung(en) (*f(pl)*)
off-the- — training	Training (*n*) durch Teilnahme (*f*) an externen Seminaren (*npl*)
on-the- — training	Ausbildung (*f*) am Arbeitsplatz (*m*)
jobbing	Börsen-, Effektenhandel (*m*)
joint	
— consultation	gemeinsame Beratung (*f*)
— negotiation	gemeinsame Verhandlung (*f*)
— representation	gemeinsame Vertretung (*f*)
— venture	gemeinsames Risiko (*n*), Gemeinschaftsunternehmen (*n*), Joint Venture (*n*)
— companies	an einem Gemeinschaftsunternehmen (*n*) beteiligte Gesellschaften (*fpl*)
jurisdiction	Zuständigkeit (*f*), Gerichtsbarkeit (*f*)

K

know-how	Know-How (*n*)

L

labour	
— dispute	Arbeitskonflikt (*m*)
— intensive	arbeitsintensiv
— mobility	Mobilität (*f*) der Arbeitskräfte (*fpl*)
— relations	Arbeitgeber-Arbeitnehmer-Verhältnis (*n*)
— turnover	Fluktuation (*f*) der Arbeitskräfte (*fpl*)
dilution of —	Einstellung (*f*) ungelernter Arbeitskräfte (*fpl*)

language

direct —	Fertigungs-, Fabrikationslohn (*m*), unmittelbar geleistete Arbeitszeit (*f*)
indirect —	Gemeinkostenlöhne (*mpl*)

language

common —	einheitlicher Code, Standardcode (*m*), gemeinsame Sprache (*f*)
computer —	Maschinensprache, Computer-Sprache (*f*)
machine —	Maschinensprache, Computer-Sprache (*f*)
lag response	verspätete Reaktion (*f*)
launching	Einführung (*f*)
lay-off	Entlassung (*f*)

lay-out

functional —	funktionale Aufteilung (*f*)
plant — study	Untersuchung (*f*) der Betriebsanlagen (*fpl*)
process equipment —	Betriebsanlage (*f*) nach Werkstattprinzip (*n*)
lead time	Anlauf-, Vorbereitungszeit (*f*), Liefer-, Auftragsbearbeitungszeit (*f*)

leader

— merchandising	Kundenwerbung (*f*) durch Sonderangebote (*npl*)
loss —	Lockvogelangebot (*n*)
market —	Marktführer (*m*)
price —	Preisführer (*m*)
leadership	Führungsrolle (*f*)

learning

— curve	Lernkurve (*f*)
programmed —	programmiertes Lernen (*n*), programmierter Lernprozess (*m*)
lease or buy	Miete (*f*) oder Kauf (*m*)

leasing

equipment —	Maschinenmiete (*f*)
leverage	Beeinflussbarkeit, Hebelwirkung (*f*)
liabilities	Verbindlichkeiten (*fpl*)
current —	laufende, kurzfristige Verbindlichkeiten (*fpl*)

licensing

crosslicensing —	Lizenzaustausch (*m*)

life

— cycle of a product	Lebenszyklus (*m*) eines Produktes (*n*)
economic —	Wirtschaftsleben (*n*)

product —	wirtschaftliche Lebensdauer (*f*) eines Produktes (*n*)
— expectancy	Lebenserwartung (*f*) eines Produktes (*n*)
line	
— and staff	Linie (*f*) und Stab (*m*)
— assistant	Linienassistent (*m*)
— authority	Linienbefugnis (*f*), Linienvollmacht (*f*)
— executive	Linienführungskraft (*f*)
— management	Linien-Management (*n*)
— manager	Linien-Manager (*m*), Linienführungskraft (*f*)
— of command	Weisungs-, Führungsstruktur (*f*), Instanzenzug (*m*)
— organisation	Linienorganisation (*f*)
— production	Fließbandproduktion (*f*)
assembly —	Fließband (*n*)
down the —	auf nachgeordneten Führungsebenen (*fpl*)
flow	Produktionsfluß (*m*)
on- —	an ein System (*n*) angeschlossen, mitlaufend, on-line
product	Produkt-, Produktionsprogramm (*n*)
linear	
— programming	lineare Programmierung (*f*)
— responsibility	lineare Verantwortung (*f*), Verantwortlichkeit (*f*)
liquid assets	liquide Mittel, flüssige Mittel (*npl*)
liquidating	
self —	sich automatisch abdeckend, zum Selbstkostenpreis (*m*)
— credit	*ein Kredit, der sich selbst liquidiert
liquidation	Liquidierung (*f*)
liquidity ratio	Liquiditätskennziffer (*f*)
load	
— factor	Auslastungsfaktor (*m*)
work —	Arbeitsanfall (*m*)
loan capital	Anleihekapital (*n*)
location	
plant —	Standort des Betriebes (*m*)
lockout	Aussperrung (*f*)
logistic process	logistisches Verfahren (*n*)
logistics	Logistik (*f*)

37

long range/term planning	langfristige Planung (*f*)
loop	
closed —	Rückkopplungssystem (*n*)
loss	
— leader	Lockvogelangebot (*n*)
— maker	verlustbringendes Produkt (*n*)
loyalty	
brand —	Markentreue (*f*)

M

MBO (management by objectives)	Führung (*f*) durch Vorgabe (*f*) von Zielen (*npl*)
MIS (management information system)	Management-Informationssystem (*n*)
MRA (multiple regression analysis)	multiple Regressionsanalyse (*f*)
machine language	Maschinensprache, Computer-Sprache (*f*)
mail	
direct —	Postversandwerbung (*f*)
maintenance	
planned —	geplante Instandhaltung (*f*), geplante Wartung (*f*)
preventive —	vorsorgliche Instandhaltung (*f*)
resale price — (RPM)	Preisbindung (*f*) der zweiten Hand (*f*)
majority interest	Mehrheitsbeteiligung (*f*)
make-or-buy-decision	Wahl (*f*) zwischen Eigenfertigung (*f*) und Kauf (*m*)
manage (to)	führen, leiten, lenken, verwalten
managed	
— costs	kontrollierte Kosten (*pl*)
system — company	nach Systemen (*npl*) geführtes Unternehmen (*n*)
management	Unternehmensführung (*f*), -lenkung (*f*), -leitung (*f*)
— accounting	Betriebsrechnungswesen (*n*)
— audit	Betriebsrechnungsprüfung (*f*)
— by exception	Eingreifen (*n*) nur bei Abweichungen (*fpl*)
— by objectives (MBO)	Führung (*f*) durch Vorgabe (*f*) von Zielen (*npl*)
— chart	Organogramm (*n*) der Unternehmensführung, der Unternehmensleitung (*f*)
— consultant	Unternehmensberater (*m*)

— development	Entwicklung (*f*) der (von) Führungskräfte(n) (*fpl*), Führungskräfteentwicklung (*f*)
— game	Unternehmens-, Führungsspiel (*n*)
— information	Management-Information(en) (*f(pl)*)
— system (MIS)	Management-Informations-system (*n*)
— potential	Führungskräftepotential (*n*)
— practices	Führungsverfahren (*npl*)
— ratio	Finanzkennziffer (*f*)
— science	Wissenschaft (*f*) (von) der Unternehmens-, Betriebsführung (*f*)
— services	Management-Dienste (*mpl*)
— succession	Führungsnachfolge (*f*), -nachwuchs (*m*)
— system	Management-System (*n*)
integrated —	integriertes Management-System (*n*)
— team	Führungsteam (*n*)
— techniques	Führungsmethoden (*fpl*), -methodik (*f*)
— theory	Management-Theorie (*f*)
business —	Betriebsführung, -wirtschaft (*f*)
cash —	Verwaltung (*f*) der liquiden Mittel (*npl*)
credit —	Kreditverwaltung (*f*)
divisional —	Spartenleitung (*f*)
dynamic — model	dynamisches Management-Modell, dynamisches Führungs-modell (*n*)
effectiveness —	wirksame Unternehmensführung (*f*)
financial —	Finanzverwaltung (*f*)
functional —	funktionales Management (*n*)
general —	allgemeines Management (*n*)
intuitive —	intuitive Unternehmensführung (*f*)
investment —	Verwaltung (*f*) von Kapitalan-lagen (*fpl*)
line —	Linien-Management (*n*)
manpower —	Menschenführung, Personal-führung (*f*)
market —	Verkaufsleitung (*f*)
matrix —	Matrix-Management (*n*)
middle —	mittleres Management (*n*)

multiple —	Unternehmensführung (*f*) unter Beteiligung (*f*) nachgeordneter Führungsebenen (*fpl*)
office —	Büroleitung (*f*)
operating —	Betriebsleitung (*f*)
operations —	operatives Management (*n*)
participative —	Management (*n*) nach dem Kollegialprinzip (*n*)
personnel —	Personalleitung (*f*)
physical distribution —	innerbetriebliche Warenverteilung (*f*)
portfolio —	Portefeuilleverwaltung (*f*)
product —	Produkt-Management (*n*)
production —	Produktionsleitung (*f*)
programmed —	programmiertes Management (*n*), Führung (*f*) durch Vorgabe (*f*) von Programmen (*npl*)
project —	Projekt-Management (*n*)
integrated — (IPM)	integriertes Projekt-Management (*n*)
sales —	Verkaufsleitung (*f*)
scientific —	wissenschaftliche Betriebsführung (*f*), wissenschaftliches Management (*n*)
staff —	Stabsleitung (*f*)
supervisory —	Kontrollfunktionen (*fpl*) des Managements (*n*), der Unternehmensleitung (*f*)
systems —	Systemverwaltung (*f*), System-Management (*n*)
top —	Unternehmensleitung (*f*)
— approach	Vorgehen (*n*) der Unternehmensleitung (*f*)
venture —	risikobereite Unternehmensführung, -leitung (*f*)
manager	Manager (*m*), Führungskraft (*f*)
advertising —	Werbeleiter (*m*)
assistant —	stellvertretender Geschäftsleiter, Direktor (*m*)
assistant to —	Direktionsassistent (*m*)
brand —	Marken-Manager (*m*), Markenbetreuer (*m*)
deputy —	stellvertretender Manager (*m*), stellvertretender Direktor (*m*)
distribution —	Vertriebsleiter (*m*)
general —	Generaldirektor (*m*)
line —	Linienführungskraft (*f*), Linien-Manager (*m*)

first —	Führungskraft (*f*) der untersten (Führungs-)Ebene (*f*)
marketing —	Marketing-Leiter (*m*)
personnel —	Personalleiter (*m*)
plant —	Werksleiter, Betriebsleiter (*m*)
product —	Produkt-Manager (*m*)
production —	Produktionsleiter (*m*)
purchasing —	Einkaufsleiter (*m*)
sales —	Verkaufsleiter (*m*)
works —	Werksleiter, Betriebsleiter (*m*)
managerial	
— control	Führungskontrolle, Kontrolle (*f*) durch Unternehmensleitung (*f*)
— effectiveness	wirksame Unternehmensleitung (*f*), -führung (*f*)
— function	Führungsfunktion (*f*)
— grid	Ausbildungsmethode (*f*) für Führungskräfte (*fpl*)
— structure	Führungsstruktur (*f*)
— style	Führungsstil (*m*)
managing director	Generaldirektor (*m*)
deputy —	stellvertretender Generaldirektor (*m*)
manpower	
— audit	Überprüfung (*f*) des Personalbestandes (*m*)
— forecasting	Prognose (*f*) des Personalbedarfes (*m*)
— management	Personalführung, Menschenführung (*f*)
— planning	Personalplanung (*f*)
— resourcing	Personalbeschaffung (*f*)
executive — strategy	Führungskräftestrategie (*f*)
manufacturing	
— capacity	Fertigungskapazität, Produktivitätskapazität (*f*)
— control	Fertigungskontrolle, Produktionskontrolle (*f*)
economic — quantity	wirtschaftliche Produktionsmenge (*f*)
margin	
gross —	Bruttogewinn (*m*), Bruttomarge (*f*)
hold —s (to)	Gewinnmargen halten
net —	Nettogewinn, Reingewinn (*m*), Nettomarge (*f*)

marginal

profit —	Gewinnspanne (*f*), Gewinn- marge (*f*)
marginal	
— analysis	Marginalanalyse (*f*)
— cost	Marginalkosten, Grenz- kosten (*pl*)
— costing	Grenzkostenrechnung (*f*)
market	
— appraisal	Marktbeurteilung (*f*)
— dynamics	Marktdynamik (*f*)
— exploration	Markterkundung (*f*)
— forces	Marktkräfte (*fpl*)
— forecast	Marktprognose (*f*)
— intelligence	Marktinformationen (*fpl*)
— leader	Marktführer (*m*)
— management	Verkaufsleitung (*f*)
— opportunity	Marktmöglichkeit (*f*)
— penetration	Marktdurchdringung (*f*)
— plan	Marktplan, Absatzplan (*m*)
— potential	Marktpotential (*n*)
— price	Marktpreis (*m*)
— profile	Marktprofil (*n*)
— prospects	Konjunktur-, Marktaussichten (*fpl*)
— rating	Markteinschätzung (*f*), Markt- bewertung (*f*)
— research	Marktforschung (*f*)
— saturation	Marktsaturierung, -sättigung (*f*)
— segments	Marktsegmente (*npl*)
— segmentation	Marktaufteilung, Marktseg- mentierung (*f*)
— share	Marktanteil (*m*)
— structure	Marktstruktur (*f*)
— study	Marktuntersuchung (*f*), Markt- studie (*f*)
— survey	Marktanalyse (*f*), Marktüber- blick (*m*)
— test	Markttest (*m*)
— trend	Markttrend (*m*), Markttendenzen (*fpl*)
— value	Marktwert (*m*)
buyers' —	Käufermarkt (*m*)
fringe —	Randmarkt (*m*)
sellers' —	Verkäufermarkt (*m*)
marketing	Marketing (*n*)
— appropriation	bewilligte Marketing-Mittel (*npl*)
— budget	Marketing-Budget (*n*)
— manager	Marketing-Leiter (*m*)

— mix	Marketing-Mix (*n*)
— research	Marketing-Forschung (*f*)
— strategy	Marketing-Strategie (*f*)
creative —	kreatives Marketing (*n*)
test —	Test-Marketing (*n*)
markup	Vertriebskosten- und Gewinn-aufschlag (*m*)
mass	
— production	Massenproduktion (*f*)
critical —	kritische Masse (*f*)
materials handling	Materialwirtschaft (*f*), Trans-portwesen, innerbetriebliches Förderwesen (*n*)
mathematical programming	mathematische Programmierung (*f*)
matrix management	Matrix-Management (*n*)
maximisation	
profit —	Gewinnmaximierung (*f*)
mean	Mittelwert (*m*)
measurement	
performance —	Leistungsmessung (*f*)
productivity —	Produktivitätsmessung (*f*)
work —	Arbeits-, Leistungsmessung (*f*), Zeitstudie (*f*), Arbeitsablauf-studie (*f*)
clerical — (CWM)	Leistungsbewertung (*f*) des Büropersonals (*n*), Leistungs-beurteilung (*f*) der Büroange-stellten (*mpl*)
media	Mittel (*npl*), Träger (*mpl*), Media (*npl*)
— analysis	Mediaanalyse (*f*)
— selection	Wahl (*f*) der Werbemittel (*npl*)
advertising —	Werbemittel (*npl*), Werbeträger (*mpl*)
median	Zentralwert (*m*)
mediation	Vermittlung (*f*)
meeting	
board —	Aufsichtsratssitzung (*f*)
memory	Speicher (*m*)
merchandising	Merchandising (*n*)
leader —	Kundenwerbung (*f*) durch Sonderangebote (*npl*)
merger	Zusammenschluß (*m*), Fusion (*f*)
merit rating	Leistungseinstufung (*f*), -beurteilung (*f*)

message	
advertising —	Werbebotschaft (*f*)
methectics	Gruppendynamik (*f*)
method	
—s engineering	Methodentechnik (*f*), Methodik (*f*)
—s study	Untersuchung (*f*) der Methodik (*f*), der Methoden (*fpl*)
critical path — (CPM)	Methode (*f*) des kritischen Pfades (*m*)
organisation and —s (O & M)	Organisation (*f*) und Methoden (*fpl*)
points rating —	Bewertungsmethode (*f*) nach Punkten (*mpl*), Beurteilungsverfahren (*n*) nach Punkten (*mpl*)
present value —	Methode (*f*) des gegenwärtigen Wertes (*m*)
random observation —	Methode (*f*) der Arbeitsstichproben (*fpl*)
simplex —	Simplex-Methode (*f*)
time and —s study	Zeit- und Bewegungsstudie, Refa-Studie (*f*)
middle management	mittleres Management (*n*)
minority interest	Minderheitsbeteiligung (*f*)
mission	
economic —	wirtschaftlicher Auftrag (*m*)
mix	
investment —	Investitionsportefeuille (*n*)
marketing —	Marketing-Mix (*n*)
product —	Produktsortiment, Warensortiment (*n*)
promotional —	die verschiedenen verkaufsfördernden Maßnahmen (*fpl*), Verkaufsförderungsmix (*n*), Verkaufsförderungspaket (*n*)
sales —	die verschiedenen Absatzmethoden (*fpl*), Verkaufsprogramm (*n*)
mobility	
labour —	Mobilität (*f*) der Arbeitskräfte (*fpl*)
staff —	vielseitige Verwendbarkeit (*f*) des Personals (*n*), der Mitarbeiter (*mpl*)
mode	Modalwert (*m*)
model	Modell (*n*)
accounting —	Buchhaltungsmodell (*n*), Kostenrechnungsart (*f*)

corporate —	Unternehmensmodell (*n*)
decision —	Entscheidungsmodell (*n*)
dynamic manage- ment —	dynamisches Führungsmodell, dynamisches Management- Modell (*n*)
modular production	Produktion (*f*) nach dem Baukastenprinzip (*n*)
monitor (to)	überwachen, kontrollieren
morphological analysis	morphologische Analyse (*f*)
motion	
— economy	Bewegungsökonomie (*f*)
— study	Bewegungsstudie (*f*)
time and —	Zeit- und Bewegungsstudie (*f*), Refa-Studie (*f*)
predetermined — time system (PMTS)	vorgegebenes System (*n*) zur Messung (*f*) von Bewegung (*f*) und Zeit (*f*)
motivation	
self —	Selbstmotivierung (*f*)
motivational research	Motivationsforschung (*f*)
motivator	Motivationsfaktor (*m*)
motive	
profit —	Gewinnmotiv, Gewinnstreben (*n*)
multi access	mehrfacher Zugang (*m*)
multiple	
— management	Unternehmensführung (*f*) unter Beteiligung (*f*) nachgeordneter Führungsebenen (*fpl*)
— regression analysis (MRA)	multiple Regressionsanalyse (*f*)

N

NPV (net present value)	gegenwärtiger Nettowert (*m*)
needs analysis	Bedarfsanalyse (*f*)
negotiation	
— strategy	Verhandlungsstrategie (*f*)
joint —(s)	gemeinsame Verhandlungen (*fpl*)
net	
— assets	Nettovermögen (*n*)
— current assets	Nettowert (*m*) des Umlauf- vermögens (*n*), Nettoumlauf- vermögen (*n*)
— margin	Rein-, Nettogewinn (*m*), Netto- marge (*f*)
— present value (NPV)	gegenwärtiger Nettowert (*m*)

network

— profit	Nettogewinn (*m*)
— worth	Eigenkapital, Gesellschafts- vermögen (*n*)

network

— analysis	Netzanalyse (*f*)
communications —	Kommunikationsnetz (*n*)
distribution —	Vertriebsnetz (*n*)
information —	Informationsnetz (*n*)
new product development	Entwicklung (*f*) neuer Produkte (*npl*)
non-executive director	nicht geschäftsführender Direktor (*m*)
non-linear program- ming	nichtlineare Programmierung (*f*)
non-profit making	gemeinnützig
numerical control	numerische Kontrolle (*f*)

O

O & M (organisation and methods)	Organisation (*f*) und Methoden (*fpl*)
OR (operational research) (operations research)	Operations Research, Unter- nehmensforschung (*f*)
objective	Ziel (*n*), Zielsetzung (*f*)
— setting	Zielsetzung (*f*)
company —(s)	Unternehmensziel(e) (*n(pl)*)
overall —s	gesamte Unternehmensziele (*npl*), Gesamtziele (*npl*) des Unternehmens (*n*)
management by —s (MBO)	Führung (*f*) durch Vorgabe (*f*) von Zielen (*npl*)
performance against —s	Soll-/Ist-Vergleich (*m*)
observation	
random — method	Methode (*f*) der Arbeitsstich- proben (*fpl*)
obsolescence	Obsoleszenz (*f*), Veralterung (*f*)
planned —	geplante, beabsichtigte Veralter- ung (*f*), geplante, beabsichtigte Obsoleszenz (*f*)
off-the-job training	Training (*n*) durch Teilnahme (*f*) an externen Seminaren (*npl*)
office	
— management	Büroleitung (*f*)
branch —	Zweigstelle, Filiale, Niederlas- sung (*f*)
head —	Zentrale (*f*), Hauptbüro (*n*)

officer	
training —	Trainingsleiter, Lehrgangsleiter (*m*)
official strike	offizieller Streik (*m*)
on-cost	Regiekosten (*pl*), Kostenzuschlag (*m*), allgemeine Handlungskosten (*pl*)
on-line	an ein System (*n*) angeschlossen, mitlaufend, on-line
on-the-job training	Ausbildung (*f*), Training (*n*) am Arbeitsplatz (*m*)
operating	
— division	Betriebsabteilung, operative Sparte (*f*)
— management	Betriebsleitung (*f*)
operational	
— planning	Betriebsplanung, operative Planung (*f*)
— research (OR)	OR, Unternehmensforschung (*f*)
operations	
— audit	Betriebsrevision (*f*), Betriebsprüfung (*f*)
— breakdown	Aufgliederung (*f*) des Stelleninhaltes (*m*)
— management	Operatives Management (*n*)
— research (OR)	OR, Unternehmensforschung (*f*)
ancillary —	Hilfsoperationen, Nebenoperationen (*fpl*)
hedging —	Hedge-Geschäft, Sicherungsgeschäft (*n*)
opportunity	
— cost	alternative Kosten (*pl*)
market —	Marktmöglichkeit (*f*)
optimisation	
profit —	Gewinnoptimierung (*f*)
optimise (to)	optimieren
option	
stock — plan	Aktienbezugsrechtsplan (*m*)
order	
economic — quantity	wirtschaftliche Losgröße (*f*)
organisation	Organisation (*f*)
— and methods (O & M)	Organisation (*f*) und Methoden (*fpl*)
— chart	Organisationsplan (*m*), Organogramm (*n*)
— planning	Organisationsplanung (*f*)
— structure	Organisationsstruktur (*f*)
— theory	Organisationstheorie (*f*)

functional —	funktionale Organisation (f)
informal —	informelle Organisation (f)
line —	Linienorganisation (f)
staff —	Stabsorganisation (f)
organisational	
— behaviour	Verhalten (n) in der Organisation (f)
— change	organisatorische Änderung (f)
— development	organisatorische Entwicklung (f), organisatorische Aufbau (m), Entwicklung (f) der Organisation (f)
— effectiveness	organisatorische Wirksamkeit (f)
organogram	Organogramm (n)
orientation	
customer —	Kundenausrichtung (f)
outlook	
profit —	Gewinnaussichten (fpl)
output	Produktion (f), Leistung (f)
— budgeting	Output-Investitionsportefolio (n), Budgetierung (f) im Produktionsbereich (m)
capital — ratio	Input-Output-Verhältnis (n) des Investitionsportefolios (n), Kapital-/Produktionsverhältnis (n), -relation (f)
computer —	Computer-Ausgabe (f)
input- — analysis	Input-Output-Investitionsportefolioanalyse, Input-Output-Analyse (f)
input- — table	Input-Output-Investitionsportefoliotabelle, Input-Output-Tabelle (f)
outside director	*dem Unternehmen (n) nicht unmittelbar zugehöriger Direktor (m)
overcapitalised	überkapitalisiert
overall company objectives	gesamte Unternehmensziele (npl), Gesamtziele (npl) des Unternehmens (n)
overheads	Gemeinkosten (pl)
— recovery	Aufteilungsverfahren (n) für Gemeinkosten (pl)
administrative —	Verwaltungsgemeinkosten (pl)
factory —	Fabrikgemeinkosten (pl)

P

P/E (price-earnings ratio)	Aktienpreis/Ertragsrelation (f), Aktienpreis/Ertragsverhältnis (n)

PERT (programme evaluation and review technique)	Methode (*f*) zur Programm-bewertung (*f*) und -überprüfung (*f*)
PMTS (predetermined motion time system)	vorgegebenes System (*n*) zur Messung (*f*) von Bewegung und Zeit (*f*)
PPBS (planning-pro-gramming-budgeting system)	Planungs-, Programmierungs-(und) Budgetierungssystem (*n*)
PR (public relations)	Öffentlichkeitsarbeit (*f*)
P/V (profit-volume ratio)	Gewinn-/Umsatzrelation (*f*), -verhältnis (*n*)
package	
— deal	Kopplungsgeschäft (*n*)
programme —	Programmpaket (*n*)
packaging	Verpackung (*f*)
palletisation	Zusammenfassung (*f*) in Paletten (*fpl*)
panel	
consumers' —	Verbraucherpanel (*n*)
parametric program-ming	parametrische Programmierung (*f*)
parent company	Muttergesellschaft (*f*)
part analysis training	Ausbildung (*f*) in Teilanalysen (*fpl*)
participation	Beteiligung (*f*), Mitwirkung (*f*)
worker —	Mitbestimmung (*f*)
participative manage-ment	Management (*n*) nach dem Kollegialprinzip (*n*)
partners	Partner, Gesellschafter, Teil-haber (*mpl*)
partnership	Partnerschaft (*f*)
party	
working —	Arbeitsgemeinschaft (*f*), Arbeits-gruppe (*f*)
patent	
— trading	Patenthandel (*m*)
payback	
— period	Amortisationszeit, -dauer (*f*)
pay off (to)	sich rentieren, sich lohnen, sich bezahlt machen
pay-off	Rentabilität (*f*), Gewinn (*m*)
payment by results	leistungsorientierte, -gerechte, -bezogene Vergütung (*f*)
payroll	Gehaltsverzeichnis (*n*), Lohnliste (*f*)
penetration	
market —	Marktdurchdringung (*f*)

per share earnings	Ertrag, Gewinn (*m*) pro Aktie (*f*)
performance	
— against objectives	Soll-/Ist-Vergleich (*m*)
— appraisal	Leistungsbewertung, -beurteilung (*f*)
— budgeting	Leistungsplanung (*f*)
— evaluation	Leistungsbewertung (*f*)
— measurement	Leistungsmessung (*f*)
— rating	Leistungseinstufung, -beurteilung (*f*)
— standards	Leistungsmassstäbe (*mpl*), -vorgabe (*f*)
earnings —	Ertragsleistung (*f*)
job —	Leistung (*f*) in der/einer Stelle (*f*)
product —	Produktleistung (*f*)
profit —	Gewinnleistung (*f*)
standard —	Vorgabeleistung (*f*)
peripheral equipment	Peripheriegeräte (*npl*)
perpetual inventory	fortlaufende Lagerbestandsaufnahme (*f*)
personal growth	persönliche Weiterentwicklung (*f*)
personnel	
— department	Personalabteilung (*f*)
— management	Personalleitung (*f*)
— manager	Personalleiter (*m*)
— policy	Personalpolitik (*f*)
— promotion	Beförderung (*f*) (von Mitarbeitern (*mpl*))
— rating	Personalbeurteilung (*f*)
— specification	Qualifikationsprofil (*n*)
pertinence tree	Zuständigkeitsbaum (*m*)
philosophy	
company —	Unternehmensphilosophie (*f*)
physical distribution management	innerbetriebliche Warenverteilung (*f*)
picket	Streikposten (*m*)
pie chart	Kreisdiagramm (*n*)
piecework	Stückarbeit (*f*)
pilot production	Versuchsproduktion, Testproduktion (*f*)
pioneer (to)	Pionierarbeit (*f*) leisten
pioneer product(s)	Pionierprodukt(e) (*n(pl)*)
plan	
action —	Aktionsplan, Durchführungsplan (*m*)
market —	Marktplan, Absatzplan (*m*)

share of production —	Produktionsanteilsplan, Anteil (*m*) am Produktionsplan (*m*)
stock option —	Aktienbezugsrechtsplan (*m*)
tactical —	taktischer Plan (*m*)
planned	
— maintenance	geplante Instandhaltung (*f*), geplante Wartung (*f*)
— obsolescence	geplante, beabsichtigte Obsoleszenz (*f*), geplante, beabsichtigte Veralterung (*f*)
planning	Planung (*f*)
— department	Planungsabteilung (*f*)
— -programming- budgeting system (PPBS)	Planungs-, Programmierungs- (und) Budgetierungssystem (*n*)
career —	Karriereplanung (*f*)
company —	Unternehmensplanung (*f*)
corporate —	Unternehmensplanung (*f*)
departmental —	Abteilungsplanung (*f*)
distribution —	Vertriebsplanung (*f*)
financial —	Finanzplanung (*f*)
forward —	Vorwärtsplanung (*f*)
long range/term —	langfristige Planung (*f*)
manpower —	Personalplanung (*f*)
operational —	Betriebsplanung (*f*), operative Planung (*f*)
organisation —	Organisationsplanung (*f*)
product —	Produktplanung (*f*)
production —	Produktionsplanung (*f*)
— and control	Produktionsplanung und -kontrolle. (*f*)
profit —	Gewinnplanung (*f*)
project —	Projektplanung (*f*)
sales —	Absatz-, Umsatzplanung (*f*)
short term —	kurzfristige Planung (*f*)
strategic —	strategische Planung (*f*)
systems —	Systemplanung (*f*)
plant	
— bargaining	innerbetriebliche Tarifverhandlungen (*fpl*)
— capacity	Anlagenkapazität, Betriebskapazität (*f*)
— hire	Anlagenmiete (*f*)
— layout study	Untersuchung (*f*) der Betriebsanlagen (*fpl*)
— location	Standort (*m*) des Betriebes (*m*)
— manager	Betriebsleiter, Werksleiter (*m*)

playing

in — training	Training (*n*) im Betrieb (*m*), innerbetriebliches Training (*n*)
playing	
role —	Rollenspiel (*n*)
ploughback	Gewinneinbehaltung (*f*)
point	
— of sale	Verkaufsort (*m*)
—s rating method	Beurteilungsverfahren (*n*) nach Punkten (*mpl*), Bewertungsmethode (*f*) nach Punkten (*mpl*)
breakeven —	Ertrags-, Gewinn-, Kostenschwelle, Rentabilitätsschwelle (*f*)
policy	
— execution	Durchführung (*f*) der Unternehmenspolitik (*f*)
— formulation	Formulierung (*f*) der Unternehmenspolitik (*f*)
— statement	Bekanntgabe (*f*) der Unternehmenspolitik (*f*)
business —	Geschäftspolitik (*f*)
company —	Unternehmenspolitik (*f*)
distribution —	Vertriebspolitik (*f*)
dividend —	Dividendenpolitik (*f*)
investment —	Investitionspolitik (*f*)
personnel —	Personalpolitik (*f*)
pricing —	Preispolitik (*f*)
promotional —	Verkaufsförderungspolitik (*f*)
sales —	Umsatzpolitik, Absatzpolitik (*f*)
selling —	Verkaufspolitik (*f*)
pooling arrangements	Kartellabkommen (*n*), Interessengemeinschaft (*f*)
portfolio	
— management	Portefeuilleverwaltung (*f*)
— selection	Portefeuilleauswahl (*f*)
position	
competitive —	Wettbewerbsposition (*f*), -stellung (*f*)
potential	
— buyer	potentieller Käufer (*m*)
development —	Entwicklungspotential (*n*)
growth —	Wachstumspotential (*n*)
management —	Führungskräftepotential (*n*)
market —	Marktpotential (*n*)
sales —	Verkaufs-, Umsatzpotential (*n*)
power	
earning —	Ertragskraft (*f*)

practices
management —	Führungsverfahren (*npl*)
restrictive —	
(labour)	restriktive Arbeitsmethoden (*fpl*), -verfahren (*npl*)
(legal)	Wettbewerbseinschränkungen, -beschränkungen (*fpl*)
predetermined motion time system (PMTS)	vorgegebenes System (*n*) zur Messung (*f*) von Bewegung (*f*) und Zeit (*f*)
premium bonus	ertragsbezogener Bonus (*m*)
present value	
— method	Methode (*f*) des gegenwärtigen Wertes (*m*)
net — (NPV)	gegenwärtiger Nettowert (*m*)
president	Präsident (*m*)
vice —	Vize-Präsident (*m*)
pressure	Druck (*m*)
preventive maintenance	vorsorgliche Instandhaltung (*f*)
price	
— cutting	Preisunterbietung (*f*)
— determination	Preisfestsetzung (*f*)
— differential	Preisgefälle (*n*), Preisunterschied (*m*)
— -earnings ratio (P/E)	Aktienpreis/Ertragsrelation (*f*), -verhältnis (*n*)
— escalation	sich gegenseitig verstärkender Preisauftrieb (*m*)
— fixing	Preisfestsetzung (*f*)
— leader	Preisführer (*m*)
— range	Preislage (*f*), Preisskala (*f*)
— structure	Preisstruktur (*f*)
competitive —	Konkurrenzpreis, konkurrenzfähiger Preis (*m*)
cut —s (to)	Preise (*mpl*) herabsetzen, senken
market —	Marktpreis (*m*)
resale — maintenance (RPM)	Preisbindung (*f*) der zweiten Hand (*f*)
pricing	
— policy	Preispolitik (*f*)
— strategy	Preisstrategie (*f*)
transfer —	Festlegung (*f*) der Verrechnungspreise (*mpl*)
probability theory	Wahrscheinlichkeitstheorie (*f*)
problem	
— analysis	Problemanalyse (*f*)
— area	Problembereich (*m*)
— solving	Problemlösung (*f*)

procedure	Verfahren (*n*)
administrative control —s	verwaltungstechnische, administrative Kontrollverfahren (*npl*), Verfahren (*n*) zur Verwaltungskontrolle (*f*)
grievance —	Beschwerdeverfahren (*n*)
systems and —s	Systeme (*npl*) und Verfahren (*npl*)
process	
— control	Verfahrens-, Fertigungskontrolle (*f*)
— costing	Kostenrechnung (*f*) für Serienfertigung (*f*)
— equipment layout	Betriebsanlage (*f*) nach Werkstattprinzip (*n*)
decision —	Entscheidungsprozess (*m*)
flow — chart	Arbeitsablaufbogen (*m*)
logistic —	logistisches Verfahren (*n*)
production —	Produktionsprozess (*m*)
processing	
batch —	Stapelverarbeitung (*f*)
data —	Datenverarbeitung (*f*)
automatic — (ADP)	automatische Datenverarbeitung (*f*)
electronic — (EDP)	elektronische Datenverarbeitung (*f*)
information —	Informationsverarbeitung (*f*)
product	
— abandonment	Streichung (*f*) eines Produktes (*n*), von Produkten (*npl*)
— advertising	Produktwerbung (*f*)
— analysis	Produktanalyse (*f*)
— area	Produktbereich (*m*)
— conception	Produktkonzeption (*f*)
— costing	Produktkostenrechnung (*f*), Ermittlung (*f*) der Erzeugniskosten (*pl*)
— design	Produktgestaltung (*f*)
— development	Produktentwicklung (*f*)
new —	Entwicklung (*f*) neuer Produkte (*npl*)
— differentiation	Produktdifferenzierung (*f*)
— diversification	Produktdiversifizierung, Produktionsbreite (*f*)
— dynamics	Produktdynamik (*f*)
— generation	Produkterzeugung (*f*)
— group	Produktgruppe (*f*)
— image	Produktimage (*n*)

— improvement	Produktverbesserung (*f*)
— life	wirtschaftliche Lebensdauer (*f*) eines Produktes (*n*)
— expectancy	Lebenserwartung (*f*) eines Produktes (*n*)
— cycle	Lebenszyklus (*m*) eines Produktes (*n*)
— line	Produkt-, Produktionsprogramm (*n*)
— management	Produkt-Management (*n*)
— manager	Produkt-Manager (*m*)
— mix	Produkt-, Warensortiment (*n*)
— performance	Produktleistung (*f*)
— planning	Produktplanung (*f*)
— profile	Produktprofil (*n*)
— profitability	Rentabilität (*f*) des Produktes (*n*), Produktrentabilität (*f*)
— range	Produktbereich (*m*), Produktskala (*f*)
— research	Produktforschung (*f*)
— strategy	Produktstrategie (*f*)
— testing	Produkttesten (*n*)
by- —	Nebenprodukt (*n*)
— testing	Testen (*n*) des Nebenproduktes (*n*)
life cycle of a —	Lebenszyklus (*m*) eines Produktes (*n*)
pioneer —	Pionierprodukt (*n*)
production	
— complex	gesamte Produktionsanlagen (*fpl*)
— control	Produktionskontrolle (*f*)
— costs	Produktionskosten (*pl*)
— engineering	Produktionstechnik (*f*)
— management	Produktionsleitung (*f*)
— manager	Produktionsleiter (*m*)
— planning	Produktionsplanung (*f*)
— and control	Produktionsplanung und -kontrolle (*f*)
— process	Produktionsprozess (*m*)
— schedule	Produktionsplan (*m*)
— scheduling	Produktionsplanung (*f*)
— standards	Produktionsnormen (*fpl*)
— targets	Produktionsziele (*npl*)
batch —	Fabrikation (*f*) nach Losgrößen (*fpl*)
cost of —	Produktionskosten (*pl*)
flow —	Massenproduktion (*f*)

productivity

continuous —	fortlaufender Produktionsablauf (*m*)
intensive —	intensive Produktion (*f*)
line —	Fließbandproduktion (*f*)
mass —	Massenproduktion (*f*)
modular —	Produktion (*f*) nach dem Baukastenprinzip (*n*)
pilot —	Testproduktion, Versuchsproduktion (*f*)
share of — plan	Anteil (*m*) am Produktionsplan (*m*), Produktionsanteilsplan (*m*)

productivity

— agreement	Produktivitätsvereinbarung (*f*), Abkommen (*n*) über Produktivitätssteigerungen (*fpl*)
— bargaining	Lohnverhandlungen mit Produktivitätsvereinbarungen (*fpl*), Produktivitätsverhandlung (*f*)
— campaign	Produktivitätskampagne (*f*)
— drive	gezielte Bemühungen (*fpl*) um Produktivitätssteigerung (*f*), Produktivitätskampagne (*f*)
— measurement	Produktivitätsmessung (*f*)
professionalisation	Erlangung (*f*) eines professionellen Status (*m*)

profile

acquisition —	Akquisitionsprofil (*n*)
company —	Unternehmensprofil (*n*)
customer —	Kundenprofil (*n*)
market —	Marktprofil (*n*)
product —	Produktprofil (*n*)
risk —	Risikoprofil (*n*)

profit

— centre	Gewinnzentrum (*n*), Kostenträger (*m*)
— accounting	Kostenträgerrechnung (*f*)
— factor analysis	Gewinnfaktoranalyse, Analyse (*f*) der Gewinnfaktoren (*mpl*)
— goal	Gewinnziel (*n*)
— impact	Gewinnauswirkung (*f*)
— implication	Gewinnauswirkung (*f*)
— improvement	Gewinnverbesserung (*f*)
— margin	Gewinnspanne (*f*), Gewinnmarge (*f*)
— maximisation	Gewinnmaximierung (*f*)
— motive	Gewinnmotiv (*n*), Gewinnstreben (*n*)

— optimisation	Gewinnoptimierung (f)
— outlook	Gewinnaussichten (fpl)
— performance	Gewinnleistung (f)
— planning	Gewinnplanung (f)
— projection	Gewinnprojektion (f)
— sharing	Gewinnbeteiligung (f)
— strategy	Gewinnstrategie (f)
— target	Gewinnziel (n)
— -volume ratio (P/V)	Gewinn-/Umsatzrelation (f), -verhältnis (n)
cost, volume, — analysis	Kosten-/Umsatz-/Gewinn- analyse, Kosten-/Gewinn-/ Volumenanalyse (f)
gross —	Bruttogewinn (m)
net —	Nettogewinn (m)
ofitability	Rentabilität (f)
— analysis	Rentabilitätsanalyse (f)
product —	Produktrentabilität (f), Ren- tabilität (f) des Produktes (n)
ogramme	
— budgeting	Programmbudgetierung (f), Aufstellung (f) des Ist-Budgets (n)
— evaluation and review technique (PERT)	Methode (f) zur Programm- bewertung (f) und -überprüfung (f)
— package	Programmpaket (n)
development —	Entwicklungsprogramm (n)
investment —	Investitionsprogramm (n)
ogrammed	
— learning	programmiertes Lernen (n), programmierter Lernprozeß (m)
— management	programmiertes Management (n), Führung (f) durch Vorgabe (f) von Programmen (npl)
ogramming	Programmierung (f)
computer —	Programmierung (f) (des Computers (m))
dynamic —	dynamische Programmierung (f)
linear —	lineare Programmierung (f)
non- —	nichtlineare Programmierung (f)
mathematical —	mathematische Programmierung (f)
parametric —	parametrische Programmierung (f)

57

progress

planning- — - budgeting system (PPBS)	Planungs-, Programmierungs- (und) Budgetierungssystem (*n*)
scientific —	wissenschaftliche Programmie- rung (*f*)

progress
— control	Fortschrittskontrolle (*f*)
work in —	Halbfertigware(n) (*f(pl)*)

progression
salary — curve	Gehaltsprogressionskurve (*f*)

project
— analysis	Projektanalyse (*f*)
— assessment	Projektbewertung (*f*)
— management	Projekt-Management (*n*)
integrated — (IPM)	integriertes Projekt-Managemen (*n*)
— planning	Projektplanung (*f*)
capital — evaluation	Bewertung (*f*) der Investitions- planung (*f*)

projection
profit —	Gewinnprojektion (*f*)
promotion (personnel)	Beförderung (*f*) (von Mitar- beitern (*mpl*))
sales —	Verkaufsförderung (*f*)

promotional
— mix	Verkaufsförderungsmix, -paket (*n*), die verschiedenen verkaufs- fördernden Maßnahmen (*fpl*)
— policy	Verkaufsförderungspolitik (*f*)

prospects
market —	Markt-, Konjunkturaussichten (*fpl*)

psychology
industrial —	Betriebspsychologie (*f*)

public
— relations (PR)	Öffentlichkeitsarbeit (*f*)
go — (to)	an der Börse (*f*) zugelassen werden

purchasing
— manager	Einkaufsleiter (*m*)

Q

QC (quality control)	Qualitätskontrolle (*f*)
total —	umfassende Qualitätskontrolle (*f*)

quantity
economic batch —	wirtschaftliche Losgröße (*f*)

economic manu- facturing —	wirtschaftliche Produktions- menge (*f*)
economic order —	wirtschaftliche Losgröße (*f*)
queuing theory	Warteschlangentheorie (*f*)
quick assets	sofort einlösbare Guthaben (*npl*), kurzfristige Mittel (*npl*)
quota	
sales —	Absatz-, Verkaufskontingent (*n*)

R

R & D (research and development)	Forschung (*f*) und Entwicklung (*f*)
ROCE (return on capital employed)	Rendite (*f*) des eingesetzten Kapitals (*n*)
RPM (resale price maintenance)	Preisbindung (*f*) der zweiten Hand (*f*)
raising	
capital —	Kapitalbeschaffung (*f*)
random	
— access	wahlfreier Zugriff (*m*)
— observation method	Methode (*f*) der Arbeitsstich- proben (*fpl*)
— sampling	Stichprobenentnahme (*f*)
range	
price —	Preisskala (*f*), Preislage (*f*)
product —	Produktskala (*f*), Produkt- bereich (*m*)
rate of return	Rendite (*f*)
internal —	interne Rendite (*f*)
rating	
credit —	Bonität (*f*)
market —	Marktbewertung (*f*), Markt- einschätzung (*f*)
merit —	Leistungseinstufung, -beurteil- ung, -bewertung (*f*)
performance —	Leistungseinstufung, -beurteil- ung (*f*)
personnel —	Personalbeurteilung (*f*)
points — method	Beurteilungsverfahren (*n*) nach Punkten (*mpl*), Bewertungs- methode (*f*) nach Punkten (*mpl*)
ratio	
accounting —	Betriebskennziffer (*f*)
capital-output —	Kapital-/Produktionsverhältnis (*n*), -relation (*f*), Input-Output- Verhältnis des Investitionsporte- folios (*n*)

cash —	Kassenkennziffer (*f*)
cover —	Deckungsverhältnis (*n*)
current —	Liquiditätskennzahl (*f*)
debt —	Verschuldungsgrad (*m*)
financial —	Finanzkennziffer (*f*)
liquidity —	Liquiditätskennziffer (*f*)
management —	Finanzkennziffer (*f*)
price-earnings — (P/E)	Aktienpreis-/Ertragsverhältnis (*n*), -relation (*f*)
profit-volume — (P/V)	Gewinn-/Umsatzverhältnis (*n*), -relation (*f*)
rationalisation	Rationalisierung (*f*)
rationing	
capital —	Kapitalzuteilung (*f*)
real time	Realzeit, Echtzeit (*f*)
recognition	
brand —	Anerkennung (*f*) als Markenartikel (*m*) durch die Verbraucher (*mpl*)
reconstruction	
company —	Wiederaufbau (*m*), Sanierung (*f*) des Unternehmens (*n*)
recovery	
— of expenses	Aufteilungsverfahren (*n*) für indirekte Kosten (*pl*)
overhead —	Aufteilungsverfahren (*n*) für Gemeinkosten (*pl*)
recruitment	Anwerbung, Beschaffung (*f*) von Arbeitskräften (*fpl*)
redeployment	Umgruppierung (*f*) der Arbeitskräfte (*fpl*)
reduction	
cost —	Kostensenkung (*f*), Rationalisierung (*f*)
variety —	Beschränkung (*f*) des Sortiments (*n*), Standardisierung (*f*), Vereinfachung (*f*)
redundancy	überflüssige Arbeitsplätze (*mpl*)
regression analysis	Regressionsanalyse (*f*)
multiple — (MRA)	multiple Regressionsanalyse (*f*)
relations	
business —	Geschäftsbeziehungen (*fpl*)
employee —	Beziehungen (*fpl*) zu Arbeitnehmern (*mpl*)
external —	Außenbeziehungen (*fpl*)
functional —	funktionale Beziehungen (*fpl*),
human —	menschliche Beziehungen (*fpl*) im Betrieb (*m*), Betriebsklima (*n*)

industrial —	Beziehungen (*fpl*) der Sozial-partner (*mpl*) zueinander
labour —	Arbeitgeber-Arbeitnehmer Verhältnis (*n*)
public — (PR)	Öffentlichkeitsarbeit (*f*)
remuneration	Vergütung (*f*)
reorganisation	Reorganisation (*f*)
replacement cost	Wiederbeschaffungskosten (*pl*), -wert (*m*)
representation	
analogue —	Analogdarstellung (*f*)
joint —	gemeinsame Vertretung (*f*)
worker —	Vertretung (*f*) der Arbeitneh-mer (*mpl*)
reproduction target	Reproduktionsziel (*n*)
resale price main-tenance (RPM)	Preisbindung (*f*) der zweiten Hand (*f*)
research	
— and development (R & D)	Forschung und Entwicklung (*f*)
— department	Forschungsabteilung (*f*)
advertising —	Werbeforschung (*f*)
consumer —	Verbraucherforschung (*f*)
desk —	Schreibtischforschung (*f*)
economic —	Wirtschaftsforschung (*f*)
field —	Primärerhebung (*f*)
market —	Marktforschung (*f*)
marketing —	Marketing-Forschung (*f*)
motivational —	Motivationsforschung (*f*)
operational, opera-tions — (OR)	Unternehmensforschung (*f*)
product —	Produktforschung (*f*)
reserve	
contingency —	Rücklage (*f*) für unvorhergese-hene Risiken (*npl*), Eventual-rückstellungen (*fpl*)
resistance	
consumer —	Produktablehnung (*f*) durch den Verbraucher (*m*)
resource	
— allocation	Allokation (*f*) von Ressourcen (*pl*), Zuteilung (*f*) von Hilfsmit-teln (*npl*)
— appraisal	Bewertung (*f*) von Ressourcen (*pl*)
resourcing	
manpower —	Personalbeschaffung (*f*)

response
anticipating —	antizipative Reaktion (*f*)
anticipatory —	antizipatorische Reaktion (*f*)
lag —	verspätete Reaktion (*f*)

responsibility
— accounting	verantwortungsbezogene Erfassung (*f*) von Kosten (*pl*) und Leistungen (*fpl*)
allocation of —ies	Zuweisung (*f*) von Verantwortlichkeiten (*fpl*)
functional —	funktionale Verantwortlichkeit (*f*)
linear —	lineare Verantwortlichkeit (*f*), lineare Verantwortung (*f*)

restrictive practices
(labour)	restriktive Arbeitsmethoden (*fpl*), -verfahren (*npl*)
(legal)	Wettbewerbsbeschränkungen, Wettbewerbseinschränkungen (*fpl*)

restructuring	Umstrukturierung (*f*)

results
payment by —	leistungsbezogene, -gerechte, -orientierte Vergütung (*f*)
retained earnings	einbehaltener, thesaurierter Gewinn (*m*)
retirement	Pensionierung, (Amts-)Niederlegung (*f*), Rück-, Austritt (*m*)
retraining	Umschulung (*f*)

retrieval
information —	Wiedergewinnung, Archivierung (*f*) von Informationen (*fpl*)

return
— on capital	Kapitalrendite (*f*)
— employed (ROCE)	Rendite (*f*) des eingesetzten Kapitals (*n*)
— on equity	Rendite (*f*) des Eigenkapitals (*n*)
— on investment	Investitionsrendite, -rentabilität (*f*)
— on sales	Gewinnspanne (*f*), Umsatzrendite (*f*)
rate of —	Rendite (*f*)
internal — (IRR)	interne Rendite (*f*)
revaluation of assets	Neubewertung (*f*) des Anlagevermögens (*n*)

review
financial —	Überprüfung (*f*) der Finanzlage (*f*), Finanzüberprüfung (*f*)

risk	
— analysis	Risikoanalyse (*f*)
— assessment	Risikobewertung, -einschätzung (*f*)
— capital	Risikokapital (*n*)
— profile	Risikoprofil (*n*)
role	
— playing	Rollenspiel (*n*)
— set	*Rollenrepertoire (*n*) eines einzelnen
room	
board —	Sitzungsraum (*m*)
rotation	
job —	systematischer Arbeitsplatzwechsel (*m*)
routine	Routine (*f*), Unterprogramm (*n*) (EDV)
diagnostic —	Beseitigung (*f*) von Fehlerquellen (*fpl*)
routing	Festlegung (*f*) der Handelswege (*mpl*)
running expenses	laufende Ausgaben (*fpl*)

S

safety	
— bank	Sicherheitsbank (*f*)
— stock	Sicherheitsbevorratung (*f*)
salary	
— progression curve	Gehaltsprogressionskurve (*f*)
— structure	Gehaltsstruktur (*f*)
sale	
point of —	Verkaufsort (*m*)
sales	
— analysis	Umsatz-, Verkaufsanalyse (*f*)
— appeal	Verkaufsappell (*m*)
— area	Verkaufsgebiet, Absatzgebiet (*n*)
— budget	Verkaufsbudget (*n*)
— coverage	Marktabdeckung (*f*), Abdeckung (*f*) durch den Verkauf (*m*)
— department	Verkaufsabteilung (*f*)
— drive	Verkaufskampagne (*f*)
— estimate	Verkaufs-, Umsatzschätzung (*f*)
— expansion effort	Bemühungen (*fpl*) um Verkaufssteigerungen (*fpl*)
— force	Außendienst (*m*)
— forecast	Umsatzprognose (*f*)

— goal	Umsatzziel (*n*)
— management	Verkaufsleitung (*f*)
— manager	Verkaufsleiter (*m*)
— mix	die verschiedenen Absatzmethoden (*fpl*), Verkaufsprogramm (*n*)
— planning	Umsatzplanung (*f*), Absatz-planung (*f*)
— policy	Absatzpolitik, Umsatzpolitik (*f*)
— potential	Umsatzpotential, Verkaufspoten-tial (*n*)
— promotion	Verkaufsförderung (*f*)
—quota	Verkaufskontingent, Absatzkon-tingent (*n*)
— talk	Verkaufsgespräch (*n*)
— territory	Verkaufsgebiet (*n*)
— turnover	Geschäftsumsatz (*m*)
— volume	Umsatzvolumen (*n*)
after — service	Kundendienst (*m*) nach dem Verkauf (*m*), Kundenbetreung (*f*)
return on —	Gewinnspanne (*f*), Umsatzren-dite (*f*)
sampling	
activity —	Arbeitsstichproben (*fpl*)
random —	Stichprobenentnahme (*f*)
satisfaction	
consumer —	Befriedigung (*f*) der Nachfrage (*f*), der Konsumentenwünsche (*mpl*)
job —	Befriedigung (*f*) durch die Aufgabe (*f*), durch die Stelle (*f*)
saturation	
market —	Marktsättigung, Markt-saturierung (*f*)
scale	
diseconomy of —	Kostenprogression (*f*)
economy of —	Kostendegression (*f*)
scatter diagram	Streubild (*n*), Streu-, Punktedia-gramm (*n*)
schedule	Plan (*m*)
production —	Produktionsplan (*m*)
scheduling	(Zeit-)Planung (*f*)
production —	Produktionsplanung (*f*)
scheme	
bonus —	Bonusplan, Prämienplan (*m*)
incentive —	Anreizplan (*m*)

suggestion —	Vorschlagswesen (*n*)
science	
behavioural —	Verhaltensforschung (*f*)
management —	Wissenschaft (*f*) (von) der Betriebsführung, der Unternehmensführung (*f*)
scientific	
— management	wissenschaftliches Management (*n*), wissenschaftliche Betriebsführung (*f*)
— programming	wissenschaftliche Programmierung (*f*)
screen (to)	durchleuchten
search	
executive —	(An-)Werbung (*f*), Vermittlung (*f*) von Führungskräften (*fpl*)
security	
industrial —	Betriebssicherheit (*f*)
job —	sicherer Arbeitsplatz (*m*)
seeking	
goal —	Zielfindung (*f*)
segmentation	
market —	Marktsegmentierung (*f*), Marktaufteilung (*f*)
segments	
market —	Marktsegmente (*npl*)
selection	
media —	Wahl (*f*) der Werbemittel (*npl*)
portfolio —	Portefeuilleauswahl (*f*)
self	
— actualisation	Eigendynamik (*f*)
— appraisal	Selbsteinschätzung (*f*)
— financing	Selbst-, Eigenfinanzierung (*f*)
— liquidating	sich automatisch abdeckend, zum Selbstkostenpreis (*m*)
— credit	*ein Kredit, der sich selbst liquidiert
— motivation	Selbstmotivierung (*f*)
sellers' market	Verkäufermarkt (*m*)
selling	
— policy	Verkaufspolitik (*f*)
direct —	Direktverkauf (*m*)
hard —	aggressive Verkaufspolitik (*f*), aggressive Verkaufsmethoden (*fpl*)

65

soft —	neutrale Verkaufspolitik (*f*)
switch —	Kundenwerbung (*f*) durch Sonderangebote (*npl*)
semi-variable costs	sprungfixe Kosten (*pl*)
sensitivity	
— analysis	Sensitivitätsanalyse (*f*)
— training	Sensitivitätstraining (*n*)
sensitise (to)	sensibilisieren, empfindlich machen
sequential analysis	sequentielle Analyse, Folgeanaly (*f*)
series	
time —	Zeitserie (*f*)
service	
advisory —s	Beratungsdienste (*mpl*)
after-sales —	Kundenbetreuung (*f*), Kundendienst (*m*) nach dem Verkauf (*m*)
computer —s	Computer-Dienste (*mpl*)
— bureau	Computer- (Dienst-) Zentrale (*f*)
customer —	Kundendienst (*m*)
extension —s	Fortbildungsangebote (*npl*)
management —s	Management-Dienste (*mpl*)
set-up costs	Anlaufkosten (*pl*)
share	
— capital	Aktienkapital (*n*)
— of production plan	Anteil (*m*) am Produktionsplan (*m*), Produktionsanteilsplan (*m*)
earnings per —	Ertrag (*m*), Gewinn (*m*) pro Aktie (*f*)
market —	Marktanteil (*m*)
sharing	
profit —	Gewinnbeteiligung (*f*)
time- —	Time-Sharing (*n*), Datenfernübertragung (*f*)
shop	
— floor	Fabrikhalle (*f*)
— steward	Betriebsobmann (*m*)
closed —	gewerkschaftspflichtiger Betrieb (*m*)
short term planning	kurzfristige Planung (*f*)
shut down (to)	stillegen, außer Betrieb setzen
simplex method	Simplex-Methode (*f*)
simplification	
job —	Stellenvereinfachung (*f*)
work —	Arbeitsvereinfachung (*f*)
simulate (to)	simulieren
simulation	Simulation (*f*)
computer —	Computer-Simulation (*f*)

sinking fund	Tilgungsfonds, Amortisations-fonds (*m*)
sit down strike	Sitzstreik (*m*)
skills analysis	Fähigkeitsanalyse (*f*), Analyse (*f*) der Fähigkeiten (*fpl*)
smoothing exponential —	Exponentialausgleichung (*f*)
soft selling	neutrale Verkaufspolitik (*f*)
software	Software (*f*)
— broker	Zwischenhändler (*m*) für Software-Vertrieb (*m*)
— firm	Firma für Software (*f*)
sole agent	Alleinvertreter (*m*)
solving problem —	Problemlösung (*f*)
source and disposition of funds	Mittelherkunft (*f*) und -einsatz (*m*)
span — of control	Kontrollspanne (*f*)
time — of discretion	zulässige Zeitspanne (*f*), zulässiger Zeitraum (*m*) für unterdurchschnittliche Leistung (*f*)
specification job —	Stellenanforderung(en) (*f(pl)*)
personnel —	Qualifikationsprofil (*n*)
spin-off effects	Sekundärnutzen (*m*)
spirit entrepreneurial —	unternehmerische Einstellung (*f*)
staff — and line	Stab (*m*) und Linie (*f*)
— assistant	Stabsassistent (*m*)
— inspection	Untersuchung, Überprüfung (*f*) des Personals (*n*)
— management	Stabsleitung (*f*)
— mobility	vielseitige Verwendbarkeit (*f*) der Mitarbeiter (*mpl*), des Personals (*n*)
— organisation	Stabsorganisation (*f*)
— transfer	Versetzung (*f*) der Mitarbeiter (*mpl*)
staggered holidays	gestaffelter Urlaub (*m*)
standard	Standard, Maßstab (*m*), Norm (*f*)
— cost(s)	Standardkosten, Sollkosten (*pl*)
— costing	Standardkostenrechnung, Plan-kostenrechnung (*f*)
— deviation	Standard-, Normalabweichung (*f*)

— performance	Vorgabeleistung (*f*)
— time	Standardzeit, Normalzeit, Zeitnorm (*f*)
budget —	Budgetnorm (*f*)
cost —	Kalkulationsnorm (*f*)
financial —	Finanznorm (*f*)
performance —	Leistungsmaßstab (*m*), -vorgabe (*f*)
production —	Produktionsnorm (*f*)
standardisation statement	Standardisierung (*f*)
policy —	Bekanntgabe (*f*) der Unternehmenspolitik (*f*)
statistical control	statistische Kontrolle (*f*)
stimulus	
competitive —	Wettbewerbsanreiz (*m*)
stock	
— control	Lagerbestandskontrolle (*f*)
— option plan	Aktienbezugsrechtsplan (*m*)
— turnover	Lagerumschlag (*m*)
— valuation	Lagerbewertung (*f*)
buffer —	Sicherheitsbevorratung (*f*)
safety —	Sicherheitsbevorratung (*f*)
stocktaking	Lagerbestandsaufnahme (*f*)
continuous —	fortlaufende Lagerbestands-, Lager-, Bestandsaufnahme (*f*)
storage	
computer —	Speicherung (*f*) auf/im Computer (*m*)
store	Lager (*n*), (Lagerhaus (*n*))
strategic	
— interdependence	strategische Wechselbeziehung (*f*)
— planning	strategische Planung (*f*)
strategy	
— formulation	Formulierung (*f*) der (Unternehmens-)Strategie (*f*)
— implementation	Durchführung (*f*) der Strategie (*f*)
brand —	Markenstrategie (*f*)
business —	Geschäftsstrategie (*f*)
competitive —	Wettbewerbsstrategie (*f*)
corporate —	Unternehmensstrategie (*f*)
defensive —	defensive Strategie (*f*)
diversification —	Diversifizierungs-, Diversifikationsstrategie (*f*)
executive manpower —	Führungskräftestrategie (*f*)

expansion —	Expansions-, Wachstumsstrategie (f)
financial —	Finanzstrategie (f)
growth —	Wachstumsstrategie (f)
marketing —	Marketing-Strategie (f)
negotiation —	Verhandlungsstrategie (f)
pricing —	Preisstrategie (f)
product —	Produktstrategie (f)
profit —	Gewinnstrategie (f)
survival —	Überlebensstrategie (f)
user —	Benutzer-, Verbraucherstrategie (f)
streamline (to)	straffen
strike	
official —	offizieller Streik (m)
sit down —	Sitzstreik (m)
unofficial —	inoffizieller Streik (m)
wild cat —	wilder Streik (m)
structure (to)	strukturieren, gestalten
structure	
authority —	Weisungs-, Befugnis-, Authoritätsstruktur (f)
capital —	Kapitalstruktur (f)
corporate —	Unternehmensstruktur (f)
cost —	Kostenstruktur (f)
grid —	Gitterstruktur (f)
managerial —	Führungsstruktur (f)
market —	Marktstruktur (f)
organisation —	Organisationsstruktur (f)
price —	Preisstruktur (f)
salary —	Gehaltsstruktur (f)
wage —	Lohnstruktur (f)
tructuring	
work —	Arbeitsgestaltung (f)
tudy	
case —	Fallstudie (f)
feasibility —	Durchführbarkeitsstudie (f)
gap —	Abweichungsanalyse (f)
market —	Marktstudie, Marktuntersuchung (f)
methods —	Untersuchung (f) der Methoden (fpl), der Methodik (f)
time and —	Zeit- und Bewegungsstudie, Refa-Studie (f)
motion —	Bewegungsstudie (f)
time and —	Zeit- und Bewegungsstudie, Refa-Studie (f)

69

style

plant layout —	Untersuchung (*f*) der Betriebs-anlagen (*fpl*)
time —	Zeitstudie (*f*)
time and motion —, time and methods —	Zeit- und Bewegungsstudie, Refa-Studie (*f*)
work —	Arbeitsstudie (*f*)
style	
managerial —	Führungsstil (*m*)
subcontracting	Tätigkeit (*f*) eines Zulieferanten (*m*)
subliminal advertising	unterschwellige Werbung (*f*)
sub-optimisation	Suboptimierung (*f*)
subsidiary company	Tochtergesellschaft (*f*), Niederlassung (*f*)
succession	
management —	Führungsnachwuchs (*m*), -nachfolge (*f*)
suggestion scheme	Vorschlagswesen (*n*)
supervisor	Vorgesetzter (*m*)
supervisory management	Kontrollfunktionen (*fpl*) der Unternehmensleitung (*f*), des Managements (*n*)
support activities	Unterstützung (*f*)
survey	
attitude —	Verhaltensanalyse (*f*)
market —	Marktanalyse (*f*), Marktüberblick (*m*)
user —	Verbrauchererhebung (*f*), Benutzeranalyse (*f*)
survival strategy	Überlebensstrategie (*f*)
switch selling	Kundenwerbung (*f*) durch Sonderangebote (*npl*)
syndicate	Syndikat (*n*), Konsortium (*n*)
synergy	Synergie (*f*), Zusammenwirken (*n*)
system	System (*n*)
—s analysis	Systemanalyse (*f*)
—s and procedures	Systeme und Verfahren (*npl*)
—s approach	Systemvorgehen (*n*), Systemverfahren (*n*)
—s design	Systemgestaltung (*f*), Systementwicklung (*f*)
—s engineering	Systemtechnik (*f*)
— managed company	nach Systemen (*npl*) geführtes Unternehmen (*n*)
—s management	System-Management (*n*), Systemverwaltung (*f*)

—s planning	Systemplanung (*f*)
—s theory	Systemtheorie (*f*)
estimating —s costs	Systemkostenvoranschlag (*m*)
information —	Informationssystem (*n*)
computerised — (COINS)	Informationssystem (*n*) auf Computer-Basis (*f*)
management — (MIS)	Management-Informations-system (*n*)
management —	Management-System (*n*)
integrated —	integriertes Management-System (*n*)
planning-pro-gramming-budget-ing — (PPBS)	Planungs-, Programmierungs-(und) Budgetierungssystem (*n*)
predetermined mo-tion time — (PMTS)	vorgegebenes System (*n*) zur Messung (*f*) von Bewegung und Zeit (*f*)
systematise (to)	systematisch darstellen

T

T-group training	T-Gruppentraining (*n*)
TWI (training within industry)	Ausbildung (*f*) in Betriebs-methoden (*fpl*) und Arbeits-beziehungen (*fpl*)
table	
input-output- —	Input-Output-Tabelle, Input-Output-Investitionsportefolio-tabelle (*f*)
tactical plan	taktischer Plan (*m*)
tactics	
competitive —	Wettbewerbstaktik (*f*)
take off (to)	abziehen, in Abrechnung (*f*) bringen, aus dem Markt (*m*) nehmen
takeover	Übernahme (*f*)
— bid	Übernahmeangebot (*n*)
talk	
sales —	Verkaufsgespräch (*n*)
tangible assets	materielle Werte (*mpl*), greifbare Vermögenswerte (*mpl*)
target	Ziel (*n*)
— setting	Zielsetzung (*f*)
production —	Produktionsziel (*n*)
profit —	Gewinnziel (*n*)
task force	Arbeitsgruppe, -gemeinschaft (*f*)
tax	
corporation —	Körperschaftssteuer (*f*)

value added — (VAT)	Mehrwertsteuer (*f*)
taxation relief	
double —	Steuererleichterung (*f*) bei Doppelbesteuerung (*f*)
team	
management —	Führungsteam (*n*)
technique	
management —s	Führungsmethodik (*f*), -methoden (*fpl*)
programme evaluation and review — (PERT)	Methode (*f*) zur Programmbewertung (*f*) und -überprüfung (*f*)
technological forecasting	Prognose (*f*) der technologischen Entwicklung (*f*)
technology	
information —	Informationstechnologie (*f*)
tender	Angebot (*n*)
terminal	Terminal (*n*)
territory	
sales —	Verkaufsgebiet (*n*)
test	
— marketing	Test-Marketing (*n*)
aptitude —	Eignungstest (*m*)
market —	Markttest (*m*)
testing	
field —	Überprüfung (*f*) im Feld (*n*), Feld-Tests (*mpl*)
product —	Produkttest (*m*), -testen (*n*)
by- —	Testen (*n*) des Nebenproduktes (*n*)
theme	
advertising —	Werbethema (*n*)
theory	
administrative —	Verwaltungstheorie (*f*)
communication —	Kommunikationstheorie (*f*)
decision —	Entscheidungstheorie (*f*)
game —	Spieltheorie (*f*)
information —	Informationstheorie (*f*)
management —	Management-Theorie (*f*)
organisation —	Organisationstheorie (*f*)
probability —	Wahrscheinlichkeitstheorie (*f*)
queueing —	Warteschlangentheorie (*f*)
systems —	Systemtheorie (*f*)
thinking	
creative —	kreatives Denken (*n*)
throughput	Durchsatz (*m*) (einer Maschine)
thrust	
competitive —	Wettbewerbsvorstoss (*m*)

time
  — and methods/   Zeit- und Bewegungsstudie,
    motion study   Refa-Studie (*f*)
  — series   Zeitserie (*f*)
  — -sharing   Time-Sharing (*n*), Datenfern-
                         übertragung (*f*)
  — span of discretion   zulässiger Zeitraum (*m*), zulässige
                         Zeitspanne (*f*) für unterdurch-
                         schnittliche Leistung (*f*)
  — study   Zeitstudie (*f*)
down —   Ausfallzeit (*f*)
lead —   Anlauf-, Vorbereitungs-,
                         Lieferzeit, Auftragsbear-
                         beitungszeit (*f*)
predetermined mo-   vorgegebenes System (*n*) zur
    tion — system   Messung (*f*) von Bewegung (*f*)
    (PMTS)   und Zeit (*f*)
real —   Realzeit, Echtzeit (*f*)
standard —   Normalzeit, Standardzeit,
                         Zeitnorm (*f*)
top management   Unternehmensleitung (*f*)
  — approach   Vorgehen (*n*) der Unternehmens-
                         leitung (*f*)
total quality control   umfassende Qualitätskontrolle
                         (*f*)
trade association   Berufsgenossenschaft (*f*),
                         Wirtschafts-, Fach-, Arbeit-
                         geberverband (*m*)
trade-off   Alternative, Wechselwirkung,
                         Interdependenz (*f*)
trade union   Gewerkschaft (*f*)
trading
  — area   Absatz-, Handelsgebiet (*n*)
  patent —   Patenthandel (*m*)
trainee turnover   Fluktuation (*f*) der Nachwuchs-
                         kräfte (*fpl*)
training   Ausbildung, Schulung (*f*),
                         Training (*n*)
  — officer   Trainingsleiter, Lehrgangsleiter
                         (*m*)
  — within industry   Ausbildung (*f*) in Betriebs-
    (TWI)   methoden (*fpl*) und Arbeits-
                         beziehungen (*fpl*)
analytical —   analytische Ausbildung (*f*),
                         Ausbildung (*f*) in analytischem
                         Denken (*n*)

transfer

booster —	zusätzliche Schulung (*f*), zusätzliches Training (*n*)
group —	Gruppentraining (*n*), Gruppenausbildung (*f*)
in plant —	innerbetriebliches Training (*n*), Training (*n*) im Betrieb (*m*)
off-the-job —	Training (*n*) durch Teilnahme (*f*) an externen Seminaren (*npl*)
on-the-job —	Training (*n*), Ausbildung (*f*) am Arbeitsplatz (*m*)
part analysis —	Ausbildung (*f*) in Teilanalysen (*fpl*)
sensitivity —	Sensitivitätstraining (*n*)
T-group —	T-Gruppentraining (*n*)
vocational —	Berufsausbildung (*f*)
transfer	
— pricing	Festlegung (*f*) der Verrechnungspreise (*mpl*)
staff —	Versetzung (*f*) der Mitarbeiter (*mpl*)
transportation	Transport (*m*)
tree	
decision —	Entscheidungsbaum (*m*)
family —	Stammbaum (*m*)
pertinence —	Zuständigkeitsbaum (*m*)
trend	Trend (*m*)
economic —	Konjunkturtrend (*m*), Konjunkturverlauf (*m*), Wirtschaftstendenzen (*fpl*)
exponential —	exponentieller Trend (*m*)
market —	Markttrend (*m*), Markttendenzen (*fpl*)
trouble shooting	Beseitigung (*f*) von Fehlerquellen (*fpl*)
trust	
brains —	Expertenrat, wissenschaftlicher Beirat (*m*), Beratungsausschuß (*m*)
turnover	
asset —	Umschlagshäufigkeit (*f*) des Kapitals (*n*)
inventory —	Lagerumschlag (*m*)
labour —	Fluktuation (*f*) der Arbeitskräfte (*fpl*)
sales —	Geschäftsumsatz (*m*)
stock —	Lagerumschlag (*m*)
trainee —	Fluktuation (*f*) der Nachwuchskräfte (*fpl*)

U

unbundling	Entbündelung (*f*)
undercapitalised	unterkapitalisiert
unofficial strike	inoffizieller Streik (*m*)
user	
— attitude	Verbrauchereinstellung (*f*), -verhalten (*n*)
— strategy	Verbraucher-, Benutzerstrategie (*f*)
— survey	Verbrauchererhebung (*f*), Benutzeranalyse (*f*)
utilisation	
capacity —	Kapazitätsauslastung (*f*)

V

VA (value analysis)	Wertanalyse (*f*)
VAT (value added tax)	Mehrwertsteuer (*f*)
valuation	
stock —	Lagerbewertung (*f*)
value	
— added	Mehrwert, Wertzuwachs (*m*)
— tax (VAT)	Mehrwertsteuer (*f*)
— analysis (VA)	Wertanalyse (*f*)
— concept	Wertkonzept (*n*)
— engineering	Werttechnik (*f*)
asset —	Fundsvermögen (*n*), Substanzwert (*m*)
book —	Buchwert (*m*)
breakup —	Altmaterial-, Ausschlachtungswert (*m*)
market —	Marktwert (*m*)
net present — (NPV)	gegenwärtiger Nettowert (*m*)
present — method	Methode (*f*) des gegenwärtigen Wertes (*m*)
variable	
— costing	variable Kostenrechnung (*f*)
— costs	variable Kosten (*pl*)
semi- —	sprungfixe Kosten (*pl*)
variance	Varianz (*f*), Abweichung (*f*)
— analysis	Varianz-, Abweichungsanalyse (*f*)
cost —	Kostenabweichung (*f*)
variety reduction	Beschränkung (*f*) des Produktsortiments (*n*), Vereinfachung, Standardisierung (*f*)
venture	
— capital	Risikokapital (*n*)

vertical integration

— management	risikobereite Unternehmens-führung (*f*), -leitung (*f*)
joint —	gemeinsames Risiko (*n*), Gemeinschaftsunternehmen (*n*), Joint Venture (*n*)
— companies	an einem Gemeinschaftsunter-nehmen (*n*) beteiligte Gesell-schaften (*fpl*)
vertical integration	vertikale Integration (*f*)
viability	Lebensfähigkeit (*f*)
viable	lebensfähig
vice chairman	stellvertretender Vorsitzender (*m*)
vice president	Vizepräsident (*m*)
vocational	
— guidance	Berufsberatung (*f*)
— training	Berufsausbildung (*f*)
volume	Volumen (*n*), Umsatz (*m*)
cost, —, profit analysis	Kosten-/Umsatz-/Gewinn-analyse (*f*), Kosten-/Gewinn-/Volumenanalyse (*f*)
profit- — ratio (P/V)	Gewinn-/Umsatzverhältnis (*n*), -relation (*f*)
sales —	Umsatzvolumen (*n*)

W

wage	
— differential	Lohngefälle (*n*)
— structure	Lohnstruktur (*f*)
walkout	Sympathiestreik (*m*)
warehousing	(Ein-)Lagerung (*f*), Lagerhal-tung (*f*)
wild cat strike	wilder Streik (*m*)
winding up	Liquidation (*f*) (-sverfahren) (*n*), Abwicklung, Auflösung (*f*) eines Geschäfts (*n*)
window dressing	Schaufensterdekoration (*f*), Aufmachung (*f*), Bilanzver-schleierung (*f*)
work	
— by contract	Arbeit (*f*) gemäß vertraglicher Vereinbarung (*f*)
— content	Arbeits-, Stelleninhalt (*m*)
— cycle	Arbeitszyklus (*m*)
— in progress	Halbfertigware(n) (*f(pl)*)
— load	Arbeitsanfall (*m*)

— measurement	Leistungs-, Arbeitsmessung (*f*), Zeitstudie (*f*), Arbeitsablaufstudie (*f*)
clerical — (CWM)	Leistungsbeurteilung (*f*) der Büroangestellten (*mpl*), Leistungsbewertung (*f*) des Büropersonals (*n*)
— simplification	Arbeitsvereinfachung (*f*)
— structuring	Arbeitsgestaltung (*f*)
— study	Arbeitsstudie (*f*)
— to rule	Dienst (*m*) nach Vorschrift (*f*), Bummelstreik (*m*)
worker	
— participation	Mitbestimmung (*f*)
— representation	Vertretung (*f*) der Arbeitnehmer (*mpl*)
working	
— capital	Betriebskapital (*n*)
— party	Arbeitsgruppe, -gemeinschaft (*f*)
works	
— council	Betriebsrat (*m*)
— manager	Betriebsleiter, Werksleiter (*m*)
worth	
net —	Eigenkapital, Gesellschaftsvermögen (*n*)

Y

yardstick	Maßstab, Erfahrungswert (*m*), Kennziffer (*f*)
year	
financial —	Finanz-, Geschäfts-, Rechnungsjahr (*n*)
fiscal —	Wirtschafts-, Geschäfts-, Rechnungsjahr (*n*)
yield	Erlös, Ertrag (*m*)
earnings —	Erlöse (*mpl*)

Z

Z-chart	Z-Diagramm (*n*)

DEUTSCH   ENGLISC

A

Abdeckung (*f*) durch den Verkauf (*m*)	sales coverage
Abfertigung (*f*)	dispatching
Abkommen (*n*)	
— über Produktivitätssteigerung (*f*)	productivity.agreement
Kartell —	pooling arrangements
Ablauf (*m*)	
— diagramm (*n*)	flow chart
Arbeits — bogen (*m*)	flow process chart
fortlaufender Produktions —	continuous flow production
kritische — stufen (*fpl*)	critical path
Analyse (*f*) der — n —	critical path analysis (CPA)
in Abrechnung (*f*) bringen	to take off
Absatz (*m*)	
— forschung (*f*)	marketing research
— gebiet (*n*)	trading/sales area, sales territory
— kontingent (*n*)	sales quota
— plan (*m*)	sales plan, market plan
— planung (*f*)	sales planning, market planning
— politik (*f*)	sales policy
— wege (*mpl*)	channels of distribution
die verschiedenen — methoden (*fpl*)	sales mix
Abschnitt (*m*)	
Rechnungs —	accounting period
Abschreibung (*f*)	
— smöglichkeit (*f*)	depreciation allowance
Zurückstellung (*f*) für — en (*pl*)	depreciation allowance
absichern	to hedge
Abteilung (*f*)	
— splanung (*f*)	departmental planning
Betriebs —	operating division
Buchhaltungs —	accounting department
Forschungs —	research department
Personal —	personnel department
Planungs —	planning department
Rechnungs —	accounting department
technische — und Konstruktionsbüro (*n*)	engineering and design department

Verkaufs — Abweichung (*f*)	sales department
— sanalyse (*f*)	variance analysis, gap study
Eingreifen (*n*) nur bei — en (*pl*)	management by exception
Kosten —	cost variance
Normal —	standard deviation
Standard —	standard deviation
Abwesenheit (*f*)	absenteeism
Abwicklung (*f*) (eihes Geschäfts)	winding up, liquidation
abziehen	to take off
adaptive Kontrolle (*f*)	adaptive control
administrative Kontrollverfahren (*npl*)	administrative control procedures
Agent (*m*)	
Werbe —	advertising agent
aggressive	
— Verkaufsmethoden (*fpl*), -politik (*f*)	hard selling
Akquisition (*f*)	acquisition
— sprofil (*n*)	acquisition profile
Aktie (*f*)	
— nbezugsrechtsplan (*m*)	stock option plan
— nkapital (*n*)	share capital
— npreis (*m*)/Ertragsrelation (*f*), — npreis/Ertragsverhältnis (*n*)	price-earnings ratio (P/E)
Ertrag (*m*) pro — , Gewinn (*m*) pro —	per-share earnings, earnings per share
Aktion (*f*)	
— splan (*m*)	action plan
Aktiva (*pl*)	assets
aktivieren	to activate, assetise
Algorithmus (*m*)	·algorithm
Alleinvertreter (*m*)	sole agent
allgemein	
— e Handlungskosten (*pl*)	on-cost
— es Management (*n*)	general management
Allokation (*f*) der Ressourcen (*pl*)	resource allocation
Alternative (*f*)	trade-off
alternative Kosten (*pl*)	opportunity cost
Altmaterialwert (*m*)	break-up value
Amortisation (*f*)	
— sdauer (*f*), — zeit (*f*)	payback period

— sfonds (*m*), — skasse (*f*)	sinking fund
Amtsniederlegung (*f*)	retirement
Analog	
— -Computer (*m*)	analogue computer (a.c.)
— darstellung (*f*)	analogue representation
— rechner (*m*)	analogue computer (a.c.)
Analyse (*f*)	
— des Deckungsbeitrages (*m*)	contribution analysis
— der Fähigkeiten (*fpl*)	skills analysis
— der Gewinnfaktoren (*mpl*)	profit factor analysis
— der kritischen Ablaufstufen (*fpl*), — des kritischen Pfades (*m*)	critical path analysis (CPA)
— der Rentabilitätsschwelle (*f*)	breakeven analysis
Abweichungs —	variance analysis, gap study
Bedarfs —	needs analysis
Benutzer —	user analysis, user (attitude) survey
Bilanz —	statement analysis
Entscheidungs —	decision analysis
Fähigkeits —	skills analysis
Finanz —	financial analysis
Folge —	sequential analysis
funktionale —	functional analysis
Gewinnfaktor —	profit factor analysis
Input-Output-Investitions-portefolio — , Input-Output —	input-output analysis
Investitions —	investment analysis
Konkurrenz —	competitor analysis
Kosten —	cost analysis
Kosten-/Gewinn-/Volumen — , Kosten-/Umsatz-/Gewinn —	cost, volume, profit analysis
Kosten-/Nutzen —	cost-benefit analysis (CBA)
Marginal —	marginal analysis
Markt —	market analysis, survey
Media —	media analysis
morphologische —	morphological analysis
Netz —	network analysis
Problem —	problem analysis
Produkt —	product analysis
Projekt —	project analysis
Regressions —	regression analysis
multiple —	multiple regression analysis (MRA)
Rentabilitäts —	profitability analysis

Risiko —	risk analysis
Sensitivitäts —	sensitivity analysis
sequentielle —	sequential analysis
Stellen —	job analysis
System —	systems analysis
Tiefen —	depth analysis
Umsatz —	sales analysis
Varianz —	variance analysis
Verhaltens —	attitude analysis
Verkaufs —	sales analysis
Wert —	value analysis (VA)
analytisch	
— e Ausbildung (*f*), Ausbildung (*f*) in — em Denken (*n*)	analytical training
an der Börse (*f*) zugelassen werden	to go public
an einem Gemeinschaftsunternehmen (*n*) beteiligte Gesellschaften (*fpl*)	joint venture companies
an ein System (*n*) angeschlossen	on-line
Änderung (*f*)	
organisatorische —	organisational change
Anerkennung (*f*) als Markenartikel (*m*) durch die Verbraucher (*mpl*)	brand recognition
Arbeitsanfall (*m*)	work load
Anforderung (*f*)	
Stellen — (en (*pl*))	job challenge, specification
Angebot (*n*)	tender, offer, bid
Fortbildungs — e (*pl*)	extension services
Lockvogel —	loss leader
Übernahme —	takeover bid
Anhebung (*f*)	
Stellen —	job improvement
Ankauf (*m*) offener Buchforderungen (*fpl*)	factoring
Anlage (*f*)	
— nkapazität (*f*)	plant capacity
— nmiete (*f*)	plant hire
— vermögen (*n*)	fixed assets, invested capital
Neubewertung (*f*) des — s	revaluation of assets
Betriebs — nach Werkstattprinzip (*n*)	process equipment layout
Kapital —	investment, invested capital

gesamte Produktions — n (*pl*)	production complex
Anlauf (*m*)	
— kosten (*pl*)	setup costs
— zeit (*f*)	lead time
Anleihekapital (*n*)	loan capital
Annahme (*f*),	
Produkt — durch den Verbraucher (*m*)	consumer acceptance
Anpassungskontrolle (*f*)	adaptive control
Anreiz (*m*)	
— plan (*m*)	incentive scheme
fehlender —	disincentive
Gruppen —	group incentive
negativer —	disincentive
Wettbewerbs —	competitive stimulus
Anteil (*m*)	
— am Produktionsplan (*m*)	share of production plan
Markt —	market share
Produktions — splan (*m*)	share of production plan
antizipative Reaktion (*f*)	anticipating response
antizipatorische Reaktion (*f*)	anticipatory response
Anwendung (*f*)	
experimentelle — psychologischer Erkenntnisse (*fpl*) auf menschliche Probleme (*npl*) im Betrieb (*m*)	human engineering
Anwerbung (*f*)	
(von Arbeitskräften (*fpl*))	recruitment, recruiting drive
— von Führungskräften (*fpl*)	executive search
Appell (*m*)	
Verkaufs —	sales appeal
Arbeit (*f*)	
— geber-/ — nehmer-Verhältnis (*n*)	labour relations
— geberverband (*m*)	trade association
— gemäß vertraglicher Vereinbarung (*f*)	work by contract
— sablaufbogen (*m*)	flow process chart
— sablaufstudien (*fpl*)	work measurement
— sanfall (*m*)	work load
— sbedingungen (*fpl*)	conditions of employment
— sgruppe (*f*)	task force, working party

— sinhalt (*m*)	work content
— sintensiv	labour intensive
— skonflikt (*m*)	labour dispute
— smessung (*f*)	work measurement
— sstichproben (*fpl*)	activity sampling
Methode (*f*) der — (*fpl*)	random observation method
— sstudie (*f*)	work-study
— svereinfachung (*f*)	work simplification
— szyklus (*m*)	work cycle
Ausbildung (*f*) am — splatz (*m*), Training (*n*) am — splatz (*m*)	on-the-job training
Ausbildung (*f*) in Betriebsmethoden (*fpl*) und — sbeziehungen (*fpl*)	training within industry (TWI)
Beziehungen (*fpl*) zu — nehmern (*mpl*)	employee relations
Interesse (*n*) an der —	job interest
Öffentlichkeits —	public relations (PR)
Pionier — leisten	to pioneer
restriktive — smethoden (*fpl*)	restrictive practices
sicherer — splatz (*m*), Sicherung (*f*) des — splatzes (*m*)	job security
Stück —	piecework
systematischer — splatzwechsel (*m*)	job security
überflüssige — splätze (*mpl*)	redundancy
unmittelbar geleistete — zeit (*f*)	direct labour
Vertretung (*f*) der — nehmer (*mpl*)	worker representation
Arbeitskräfte (*fpl*)	
Beschaffung (*f*) von — n (*pl*)	recruitment
Einstellung (*f*) nicht benötigter —	feather bedding
Einstellung (*f*) ungelernter —	dilution of labour
Fluktuation (*f*) der —	labour turnover
Mobilität (*f*) der —	labour mobility
Umgruppierung (*f*) der —	redeployment
Archivierung (*f*) von Informationen (*fpl*)	information retrieval
Artikel (*m*)	
Marken —	brand product
Assistent (*m*)	
Direktions —	assistant to manager
Linien —	line assistant

Stabs —	staff assistant
Aufbau (*m*)	
— der Organisation (*f*)	organisational development
auf Computer (*m*) umstellen	to computerise
Aufgabe (*f*)	assignment
Befriedigung (*f*) durch die —	job satisfaction
Herausforderung (*f*) durch die —	job challenge
Zuteilung (*f*) von — n (*pl*)	(job) assignment
Aufgliederung (*f*)	
— des Stelleninhaltes (*m*)	operations breakdown
betriebliche —	departmentalisation
Auflegung (*f*)	flotation
Auflösung (*f*) (eines Geschäfts)	liquidation, winding up
Aufmachung (*f*)	window dressing
auf nachgeordneten Führungsebenen (*fpl*)	down the line
Aufnahme (*f*)	
fortlaufende Bestands —	continuous stocktaking,
Lager — , fortlaufende Lagerbestands —	perpetual inventory
Aufschlag (*m*)	
Vertriebskosten- und Gewinn —	markup
Aufschlüsselung (*f*)	
Kosten —	allocation of costs
Aufsichtsrat (*m*)	board of directors
— skontrolle (*f*)	board control
— ssitzung (*f*)	board meeting
Schachtel —	interlocking directorate
Aufstellung (*f*) des Ist-Budgets (*n*)	programme budgeting
Aufstieg (*m*) der Führungskräfte (*fpl*)	executive advancement
Aufteilung (*f*)	
— sverfahren (*n*)	
— für Gemeinkosten (*pl*)	overheads recovery
— für indirekte Kosten (*pl*)	recovery of expenses
funktionale —	functional layout
Kosten — sverfahren (*n*)	absorption costing
Markt —	market segmentation
Auftrag (*m*)	assignment
— sbearbeitungszeit (*f*)	lead time
wirtschaftlicher —	economic mission
Ausbildung (*f*)	training
— in analytischem Denken (*n*)	analytical training
— am Arbeitsplatz (*m*)	on-the-job training

— in Betriebsmethoden (*fpl*) und Arbeitsbeziehungen (*fpl*)	training within industry (TWI)
— in Teilanalysen (*fpl*)	part analysis training
— smethode (*f*) für Führungskräfte (*fpl*)	managerial grid
analytische —	analytical training
Berufs —	vocational training
Gruppen —	group training
aus dem Markt (*m*) nehmen	to take off
Ausfallzeit (*f*)	down time
Ausführung (*f*)	
Überprüfung (*f*) nach der —	follow-up
Ausgabe (*f*)	
laufende Betriebs —	current expenditure
Computer- —	computer output
direkte — n (*pl*)	direct expenses
indirekte — n (*pl*)	indirect expenses
laufende — n (*pl*)	running expenses
ausgegebenes Kapital (*n*)	issued capital
Ausgleichung (*f*)	
Exponential —	exponential smoothing
Auslastung (*f*)	
— sfaktor (*m*)	load factor
Kapazitäts —	capacity utilisation
Ausrichtung (*f*)	
Kunden —	customer orientation
Ausschlachtungswert (*m*)	break-up value
Ausschuß (*m*)	
Beratungs —	brains trust
Außendienst (*m*)	sales force
außer Betrieb (*m*) setzen	to shut down
Aussichten (*fpl*)	
Gewinn —	profit outlook
Konjunktur — , Markt —	market prospects
Aussperrung (*f*)	lockout
ausstatten	
mit Kapital —	to capitalise
Ausstattung (*f*)	
Kapital —	gearing
Austausch (*m*)	
Lizenz —	cross-licensing
Austritt (*m*)	retirement, resignation
Auswahl (*f*)	
Portefeuille —	portfolio selection
Auswirkung (*f*)	impact
Gewinn —	profit impact, profit implication

Automation (*f*), Automatisierung (*f*)	automation
automatische Datenverarbeitung (*f*)	automatic data processing (ADP)
Autoritätsstruktur (*f*)	authority structure, line of command

B

Balkendiagramm (*n*)	bar chart
Bank (*f*)	
Computer- —	computer bank
Daten —	data bank
Sicherheits —	safety bank
Baukasten (*m*)	
Produktion (*f*) nach dem — prinzip (*n*)	modular production
Baum (*m*)	
Entscheidungs —	decision tree
Stamm —	family tree
Zuständigkeits —	pertinence tree
beabsichtigte Obsoleszenz (*f*), beabsichtigte Veralterung (*f*)	planned obsolescence
Bearbeitung (*f*)	
Informations —	information handling
Bedarf (*m*)	
— sanalyse (*f*)	needs analysis
Prognose (*f*) des Personal — es	manpower forecasting
Bedingung (*f*)	
Arbeits — en (*pl*)	conditions of employment
Beeinflussbarkeit (*f*)	leverage
Beförderung (*f*) (von Mitarbeitern (*mpl*))	(personnel) promotion
— der Führungskräfte (*fpl*)	executive advancement
Befriedigung (*f*)	
— der Konsumentenwünsche (*mpl*), — der Nachfrage (*f*)	consumer satisfaction
— durch die Aufgabe (*f*), durch die Stelle (*f*)	job satisfaction
Befugnis (*f*)	
— struktur (*f*)	authority structure, line of command
Beschränkung (*f*) der — se, von — ssen (*pl*)	contraction of authority
Linien —	line authority
Beirat (*m*)	
wissenschaftlicher —	brains trust

Beitrag (*m*)

    Analyse (*f*) des Deckungs — es   contribution analysis

Bekanntgabe (*f*) der Unter-   policy statement
    nehmenspolitik (*f*), Bekannt-
    machung (*f*) der Unter-
    nehmenspolitik

Bemühung (*f*)

    — en (*pl*) um Verkaufssteiger-   sales expansion effort
    ungen (*fpl*)

    gezielte — en (*pl*) um   productivity drive
    Produktivitätssteigerung (*f*)

Benutzer (*m*)

    — analyse (*f*)   user analysis, user
                 (attitude) survey

    — strategie (*f*)   user strategy

Berater (*m*)

    Unternehmens —   (management) consul-
                 tant

Beratung (*f*)

    — sausschuß (*m*)   brains trust

    — sdienste (*mpl*)   advisory services

    — sunternehmen (*n*)   consultancy

    Berufs —   vocational guidance

    gemeinsame —   joint consultation

    Personal —   employee counselling

Bereicherung (*f*) durch die   job enrichment
    Stelle (*f*)

Bereich (*m*)

    Problem —   problem area

    Produkt —   product area, product
                 range

    Wachstums —   growth area

Beruf (*m*)

    — sausbildung (*f*)   vocational training

    — sberatung (*f*)   vocational guidance

    — sgenossenschaft (*f*)   trade association

Berührungspunkte (*mpl*)   interface

Beschaffung (*f*)

    — von Arbeitskräften (*fpl*)   recruitment

    Daten —   data acquisition

    Kapital —   capital raising

    Personal —   manpower resourcing

Beschränkung (*f*)

    — der Befugnisse, — von   contraction of authority
    Befugnissen.(*fpl*)

    — des Sortiments (*n*)   variety reduction

    Budget —   budget constraint

Beschreibung

Wettbewerbs — en *(fpl)*	restrictive practices (legal)
Beschreibung *(f)*	
Stellen —	job description
Beschwerdeverfahren *(n)*	grievance procedure
beseitigen	
Fehler *(mpl)* —	to debug
Beseitigung *(f)* von Fehlerquellen *(fpl)*	diagnostic routine, trouble shooting
Besitz *(m)*	
— entziehung *(f)*	divestment
— stand *(m)*	assets
Besprechungen *(fpl)*	
Handels —	trade negotiations, trade talks
Bestand *(m)*	
(fortlaufende) — saufnahme *(f)*	(continuous) stocktaking, (perpetual) inventory
Besteuerung *(f)*	
Steuererleichterung *(f)* bei Doppel —	double taxation relief
Beteiligung *(f)*	affiliate company; participation
— sgesellschaft *(f)*	affiliate company
Gewinn —	profit-sharing
Mehrheits —	majority interest
Minderheits —	minority interest
Unternehmensführung *(f)* unter — nachgeordneter Führungsebenen *(fpl)*	multiple management
Betreuer *(m)*	
Marken —	brand manager
Betreuung *(f)*	
Kunden —	after-sales service
Betrieb *(m)*	factory, plant, works, firm, enterprise
außer — setzen	to shut down, put out of action
experimentelle Anwendung *(f)* psychologischer Erkenntnisse *(fpl)* auf menschliche Probleme *(npl)* im —	human engineering
gewerkschaftspflichtiger —	closed shop
menschliche Beziehungen *(fpl)* im —	human relations
Standort *(m)* des — es	plant location

Training (*n*) im —	in-plant training
betriebliche Aufgliederung (*f*)	departmentalisation
Betriebs —	
— abteilung (*f*)	operating division
— anlage (*f*) nach Werk-	process equipment
stattprinzip (*n*)	layout
— dynamik (*f*)	industrial dynamics
— führung (*f*)	business management
wissenschaftliche —	scientific management
Wissenschaft (*f*) (von) der —	management science
— kapazität (*f*)	plant capacity
— kapital (*n*)	working capital,
	circulating capital
— kennziffer (*f*)	accounting ratio
— klima (*n*)	human relations
— leiter (*m*)	works manager, plant
	manager
— leitung (*f*)	operating management
— obmann (*m*)	shop steward
— ökonom (*m*)	business economist
— psychologie (*f*)	industrial psychology
— prüfung (*f*)	operations audit
— rat (*m*)	works council
— rechnungsprüfung (*f*)	management audit
— rechnungswesen (*n*)	management accounting
— revision (*f*)	operations audit
— sicherheit (*f*)	industrial security
— studie (*f*)	industrial engineering
— vergleich (*m*)	interfirm comparison
— wirtschaft (*f*)	industrial management,
	business management
— wirtschaftler (*m*)	industrial management
	consultant, business
	analyst, business
	economist
Ausbildung (*f*) in — methoden	training within industry
(*fpl*) und Arbeitsbeziehungen	(TWI)
(*fpl*)	
laufende — ausgaben (*fpl*)	current expenditure
laufende — kosten (*pl*)	current expenditure
Untersuchung (*f*) der	plant layout study
— anlagen (*fpl*)	
Beurteilung (*f*)	assessment, evaluation,
	appraisal
— sverfahren (*n*) nach	points rating method
Punkten (*mpl*)	
Investitions —	capital expenditure
	appraisal

Leistungs —	performance evaluation, performance appraisal
— der Büroangestellten (*mpl*)	clerical work measurement (CWM)
Markt —	market appraisal, market rating
Personal —	personnel rating
Stellen —	job evaluation
Bevorratung (*f*)	
Sicherheits —	buffer stock, safety stock
Bewegung (*f*)	
— sökonomie (*f*)	motion economy
— sstudie (*f*)	motion study
Zeit- und —	time and motion study, time and methods study
vorgegebenes System (*n*) zur Messung (*f*) von — und Zeit (*f*)	predetermined motion time system (PMTS)
Bewertung (*f*)	assessment, evaluation, appraisal
— der Finanzmittel (*npl*)	financial appraisal
— der Investitionsplanung (*f*)	capital project evaluation
— smethode (*f*) nach Punkten (*mpl*)	points rating method
— von Ressourcen (*pl*)	resource appraisal
dynamische —	dynamic evaluation
Finanz —	financial appraisal
Investitions —	investment appraisal, capital expenditure appraisal
Leistungs —	performance evaluation, performance appraisal
— des Büropersonals (*n*)	clerical work measurement (CWM)
Markt —	market rating, market appraisal
Nachfrage —	demand assessment
Neu — des (Anlage-) Vermögens (*n*)	revaluation of assets
Stellen —	job evaluation
bewilligt	
— e Budgetmittel (*npl*), — es Budget (*n*), — er Budget-fonds (*m*)	budget appropriation
— e Marketing-Mittel (*npl*)	marketing appropriation

— e Werbemittel (*npl*), — er Werbeetat (*m*), — er Werbefonds (*m*)	advertising appropriation
Bewußtsein (*n*)	
Kosten —	cost awareness, cost consciousness
Marken —	brand awareness
bezahlt	
sich — machen	to pay off
Beziehungen (*fpl*)	
— der Sozialpartner (*mpl*) zueinander	industrial relations
— zu Arbeitnehmern (*mpl*)	employee relations
Ausbildung (*f*) in Betriebs- methoden (*fpl*) und Arbeits —	training within industry (TWI)
Außen —	external relations
funktionale —	functional relations
Geschäfts —	business relations
menschliche — im Betrieb (*m*)	human relations
Wechsel —	interface
strategische —	strategic interde- pendence
Bezugsrecht (*n*)	option
Aktien — splan (*m*)	stock option plan
Bilanz (*f*)	
— ierungsperiode (*f*)	accounting period
— prüfung (*f*)	audit, balance sheet auditing
— verschleierung (*f*)	window dressing
Bild (*n*)	diagram, chart
Marken —	brand image
Streu —	scatter diagram
Bildung (*f*)	
Kapital — , Vermögens —	capital formation
Bindung (*f*)	
Kapital —	capital commitment
Bonität (*f*)	credit rating
Bonus (*m*)	premium, bonus
— plan (*m*)	bonus scheme
ertragsbezogener —	premium bonus
Gruppen —	group bonus
Börse (*f*)	
— nhandel (*m*)	jobbing
an der — zugelassen werden	to go public
Botschaft (*f*)	
Werbe —	advertising message

91

Breite (*f*)	
Produktions —	product diversification
Brutto —	
— gewinn (*m*)	gross profit
— marge (*f*)	gross margin
Buchforderungen (*fpl*)	
Ankauf (*m*) offener —	factoring
Buchhalter (*m*)	
Haupt —	chief accountant
Buchhaltung (*f*)	
— sabteilung (*f*)	accounting department
— smodell (*n*)	accounting model
Buchwert (*m*)	book value
Budget (*n*)	
— beschränkung (*f*)	budget constraint
— kontrolle (*f*)	budget(ary) control
— mittel (*npl*)	budget
bewilligte —	budget appropriation
— normen (*fpl*)	budget standards
— prognose (*f*)	budget forecasting
Aufstellung (*f*) des Ist- — s	programme budgeting
bewilligter — fonds (*m*)	budget appropriation
bewilligtes —	budget appropriation
elastisches —	flexible budget
Investitions —	investment budget
Kapital —	capital budget
Kassen —	cash budget
Marketing- —	marketing budget
Verkaufs —	sales budget
Werbe —	advertising budget
Budgetierung (*f*)	
— im Produktionsbereich (*m*)	output budgeting
— skontrolle (*f*)	budgeting control
Planungs-, Program-	planning- programming-
mierungs- und — ssystem (*n*)	budgeting system (PPBS)
Kapital —	capital budgeting
Kassen —	cash budgeting
Programm —	programme budgeting
Bummelstreik (*m*)	go-slow, work-to-rule
Büro (*n*)	
— angestellte (*pl*)	personnel, office staff
— leitung (*f*)	office management
— personal (*n*)	clerical staff, office personnel
Haupt —	head office
Leistungsbeurteilung (*f*),	clerical work measure-
Leistungsbewertung (*f*) des — s	ment (CWM)

technische Abteilung (*f*) und Konstruktions —	engineering and design department

C

ash Flow (*m*)	cash flow
Differential (*n*) des —	incremental cash flow
diskontierter —	discounted cash flow (DCF)
Zuwachs (*m*) des —	incremental cash flow
ode (*m*)	
einheitlicher — , Standard —	common language
omputer (*m*)	
— -Ausgabe (*f*)	computer output
— -Bank (*f*)	computer bank
— -Dienste (*mpl*)	computer services
— -Dienstzentrale (*f*)	computer services bureau
— -Eingabe (*f*)	computer input
— -Simulation (*f*)	computer simulation
— -Sprache (*f*)	computer language
— -Zentrale (*f*)	computer services bureau
Analog- —	analogue computer (ac)
auf — umstellen	to computerise
Digital- —	digital computer
Informationssystem (*n*) auf — -Basis (*f*)	computerised information system (COINS)
Programmierung (*f*) des —s	computer programming
Speicherung (*f*) auf/im —	computer storage
ontainer (*m*)	
Umstellung (*f*) auf —	containerisation
ontroller (*m*)	comptroller, controller

D

achgesellschaft (*f*)	holding company
arstellen	
systematisch —	to systematise
arstellung (*f*)	
Analog —	analogue representation
aten (*npl*)	
— bank (*f*)	data bank
— beschaffung (*f*)	data acquisition
— fernübertragung (*f*)	time-sharing
— sammlung (*f*)	data gathering
— verarbeitung (*f*)	data processing

automatische —	automatic data processing (ADP)
elektronische —	electronic data processing (ADP)
Dauer (f)	
Amortisations —	payback period
wirtschaftliche Lebens — des Produkts	product life
Debitorenverkauf (m)	factoring
Deckung (f)	
Analyse (f) des — sbeitrages (m)	contribution analysis
— sverhältnis (n)	cover ratio
defensive Strategie (f)	defensive strategy
Degression (f)	
Kosten —	economy of scale
Delegation (f)	delegation
Denken (n)	
Ausbildung (f) im analytischen —	analytical training
kreatives —	creative thinking, brain storming
Desinvestition (f)	disinvestment
Dezentralisation (f)	departmentalisation
Dezentralisierung (f)	decentralisation
Diagramm (n)	
Ablauf —	flow chart
Balken —	bar chart
Kreis —	pie chart
Punkte —	scatter diagram
Streu —	scatter diagram
Tätigkeits —	activity chart
Z- —	Z-chart
die verschiedenen Absatzmethoden (fpl)	sales mix
die verschiedenen verkaufsfördernden Massnahmen (fpl)	promotional mix
*dem Unternehmen (n) nicht unmittelbar zugehöriger Direktor (m)	outside director
Dienst (m)	
— nach Vorschriften (fpl)	work-to-rule
Außen —	sales force
Beratungs — e (pl)	advisory services
Computer- — e (pl)	computer services
Kunden —	customer service
— nach dem Verkauf (m)	after-sales service
Management- — e (pl)	management services

Differential (*n*) des Cash Flow (*m*)	incremental cash flow
Differenzierung (*f*)	
Produkt —	product differentiation
Digital-Computer (*m*), — rechner (*m*)	digital computer
direkt	
— e Ausgaben (*fpl*)	direct expenses
— e Kosten (*pl*)	direct cost
— verkauf (*m*)	direct selling
Direktionsassistent (*m*)	assistant manager, assistant to manager
Direktor (*m*)	
*dem Unternehmen (*n*) nicht unmittelbar zugehöriger —	outside director
Finanz —	financial director
General —	managing director, chief executive, general manager, executive director
stellvertretender —	deputy managing director
geschäftsführender —	executive director
nicht —	non-executive director
stellvertretender —	deputy manager, assistant manager
diskontierter Cash Flow (*m*)	discounted cash flow (DCF)
Diversifikation (*f*)	diversification
— sstrategie (*f*)	diversification strategy
diversifizieren	to diversify
Diversifizierung (*f*)	diversification
— sstrategie (*f*)	diversification strategy
Produkt —	product diversification
Dividenden (*fpl*)	dividends
— politik (*f*)	dividends policy
Doppelbesteuerung (*f*)	
Steuererleichterung (*f*) bei —	double taxation relief
Druck (*m*)	pressure, stress
Dumping (*n*)	dumping
Durchbruch (*m*)	breakthrough
Durchdringung (*f*)	
Markt —	market penetration
Durchführbarkeitsstudie (*f*)	feasibility study
durchführen	to carry out, execute
Revision (*f*) —	to audit
Durchführung (*f*)	
— der Strategie (*f*)	strategy implementation

— der Unternehmenspolitik (*f*)	policy execution
— splan (*m*)	action plan
durchleuchten	to screen, analyse
Durchsatz (*m*) (einer Maschine (*f*))	throughput
durchschnittliche Kosten (*pl*), Durchschnittskosten (*pl*)	average cost
Dynamik (*f*)	
Betriebs —	industrial dynamics
Eigen —	self actualisation
Gruppen —	group dynamics, methectics
Industrie —	industrial dynamics
Markt —	market dynamics
Produkt —	product dynamics
dynamisch	
— e Bewertung (*f*)	dynamic evaluation
— es Führungsmodell (*n*), — es Management-Modell (*n*)	dynamic management model
— e Programmierung (*f*)	dynamic programming

E

Echtzeit (*f*)	real time
Effektenhandel (*m*)	jobbing
Effizienz (*f*)	efficiency
Eigendynamik (*f*)	self actualisation
Eigenfertigung (*f*)	
Wahl (*f*) zwischen — und Kauf (*m*)	make-or-buy decision
Eigenfinanzierung (*f*)	self financing
Eigenkapital (*n*)	equity, net worth
Rendite (*f*) des — s	return on equity
Eignungsprüfung (*f*), Eignungstest (*m*)	aptitude test
einbehaltener Gewinn (*m*)	retained earnings
Einbehaltung (*f*)	
Gewinn —	ploughback
Einführung (*f*) neuer Mitarbeiter (*mpl*) in das Unternehmen	induction
Eingabe (*f*)	input
Computer- —	computer input
eingesetztes Kapital (*n*)	capital employed
Rendite (*f*) des eingesetzten Kapitals	return on capital employed (ROCE)
Eingreifen (*n*) nur bei Abweichungen (*fpl*)	management by exception

einheitlicher Code (*m*)	common language
Einkaufsleiter (*m*)	purchasing manager
Einkäufer (*m*)	
Haupt —	chief buyer
Einlagerung (*f*)	warehousing, storage
einlösbar	
sofort — e Guthaben (*npl*)	quick assets
Einsatz (*m*)	deployment
Mittelherkunft (*f*) und	source and disposition
Mittel —	of funds
verstärkter — der Werbemittel	advertising drive
(*npl*), verstärkter Werbe —	
Einschätzung (*f*)	assessment, estimate
Markt —	market rating
Risiko —	risk assessment
Selbst —	self appraisal
Einstellung (*f*)	
— nicht benötigter Arbeits-	feather bedding
kräfte (*fpl*)	
— ungelernter Arbeitskräfte	dilution of labour
(*fpl*)	
unternehmerische —	entrepreneurial spirit
Verbraucher —	user attitude
Einstufung (*f*)	
Leistungs —	merit rating, perform-
	ance rating
Einweisung (*f*)	briefing
elastisches Budget (*n*)	flexible budget
Elastizität (*f*)	elasticity
elektronische Datenverarbeitung	electronic data
(*f*)	processing (EDP)
Emission (*f*)	flotation
— skapital (*n*)	issued capital
empfindlich machen	to sensitise
Entbündelung (*f*)	unbundling
Entfaltung (*f*)	deployment
Entnahme (*f*)	
Stichproben —	random sampling
Entscheidung (*f*)	
— sanalyse (*f*)	decision analysis
— sbaum (*m*)	decision tree
— sfindung (*f*)	decision-making
— smodell (*n*)	decision model
— sprozeß (*m*)	decision process
— stheorie (*f*)	decision theory
Entwicklung (*f*)	
— der Organisation (*f*)	organisational develop-
	ment

Entwurf

— neuer Produkte (*npl*)	new product development
— spotential (*n*)	development potential
— sprogramm (*n*)	development programme
— von Führungskräften (*fpl*)	management/executive development
Forschung (*f*) und —	research and development (R & D)
Markt —	market trends
Produkt —	product development
System —	systems design
Prognose (*f*) der technoloischen —	technological forecast
persönliche Weiter —	personal growth
Entwurf (*m*)	
Stellen —	job design
Entziehung (*f*)	
Besitz —	divestment
Erfassung (*f*)	
verantwortungsbezogene —	responsibility accounting
von Kosten (*pl*) und Leistungen (*fpl*)	
Ergonometrik (*f*)	ergonometrics
Ergonomik (*f*)	ergonomics
Erhebung (*f*)	survey
Primär —	field research
Verbraucher —	user (attitude) survey
Erkenntnis (*f*)	
experimentelle Anwendung (*f*) psychologischer — se (*pl*) auf menschliche Probleme (*npl*) im Betrieb (*m*)	human engineering
Erkundung (*f*)	
Markt —	market exploration
Erlangung (*f*) eines professionellen Status (*m*)	professionalisation
Ermittlung (*f*) der Erzeugniskosten (*pl*)	product costing
Ertrag (*m*)	
— pro Aktie (*f*)	earnings per share, pershare earnings
— sbezogener Bonus (*m*)	premium bonus
— skraft (*f*)	earning power
— sleistung (*f*)	earnings performance
— sschwelle (*f*)	breakeven point
Aktienpreis/ — srelation (*f*), — sverhältnis (*n*)	price-earnings ratio (P/E)

Vermögens — Erwartungen (*fpl*)	earnings on assets
mit einer Stelle (*f*) verbundene —	job expectations
Umsatz —	sales expectations
Verkaufs —	sales expectations
Erweiterung (*f*)	
Stellen —	job enlargement
Erwerb (*m*)	acquisition
Erzeugniskosten (*pl*)	
Ermittlung (*f*) der —	product costing
Erzeugung (*f*)	
Produkt —	product generation
Etat (*m*)	
Werbe —	advertising budget
bewilligter —	advertising appropriation
Eventualrückstellung (*f*)	contingency reserve
Expansionsstrategie (*f*)	expansion strategy
experimentelle Anwendung (*f*) psychologischer Erkenntnisse (*fpl*) auf menschliche Probleme (*npl*) im Betrieb (*m*)	human engineering
Expertenrat (*m*)	brains trust
Exponentialausgleichung (*f*)	exponential smoothing
exponentieller Trend (*m*)	exponential trend

F

Fabrik (*f*)	
— gemeinkosten (*pl*)	factory overheads
— halle (*f*)	shop floor
Fabrikation (*f*) nach Losgrößen (*fpl*)	batch production
Fachverband (*m*)	trade association
Fähigkeit (*f*)	
— sanalyse (*f*), Analyse (*f*) der — en (*pl*)	skills analysis
Führungs — en (*pl*)	executive competence
Leistungs —	efficiency
Faktor (*m*)	
Auslastungs —	load factor
Gewinn — analyse (*f*), Analyse (*f*) der Gewinn — en (*pl*)	profit factor analysis
Kosten —	cost factor
Motivations —	motivator
Fallstudie (*f*)	case study
Fehlen (*n*) der Mitarbeiter (*mpl*)	absenteeism

fehlender Anreiz (*m*)	disincentive
Fehler (*m*)	
— (*pl*) beseitigen	to debug
Beseitigung (*f*) von — quellen (*fpl*)	trouble shooting, diagnostic routine
Feld (*n*)	
— -Tests (*mpl*)	field testing
Überprüfung (*f*) im —	field testing
Feldzug (*m*)	
Werbe —	advertising drive
Fernbleiben (*n*)	absenteeism
Fertigung (*f*)	
— skapazität (*f*)	manufacturing capacity
— skontrolle (*f*)	manufacturing/production control
— slohn (*m*)	direct labour
industrielle — stechnik (*f*)	industrial engineering
Kostenrechnung (*f*) für Serien —	process costing
Festlegung (*f*)	
— der Handelswege (*mpl*)	routing
— der Verrechnungspreise (*mpl*)	transfer pricing
Festsetzung (*f*)	
Preis —	price fixing, price determination
Filiale (*f*)	branch office
Finanz (*f*)	
— analyse (*f*)	financial analysis
— bewertung (*f*)	financial appraisal
— direktor (*m*)	financial director
— jahr (*n*)	financial year, fiscal year
— kennziffer (*f*)	financial ratio, management ratios
— kontrolle (*f*)	financial control
— normen (*fpl*)	financial standards
— planung (*f*)	financial planning
— strategie (*f*)	financial strategy
— überprüfung (*f*)	financial review
— verwaltung (*f*)	financial management/administration
Bewertung (*f*) der — mittel (*npl*)	financial appraisal
Überprüfung (*f*) der — lage (*f*)	financial review
Finanzierung (*f*)	
Eigen — , Selbst —	self financing
Findung (*f*)	
Entscheidungs —	decision making

Ziel —	goal seeking
Firma (n) für Software (f)	software firm
Firmenwert (m)	goodwill
fixe Kosten (pl)	fixed costs
Fließband (n)	assembly line
— produktion (f)	line production
Fluktion (f)	
— der Arbeitskräfte (fpl)	labour turnover
— der Nachwuchskräfte (fpl)	trainee turnover
Fluß (m)	
Informations —	information flow
Produktions —	flow line
flüssige Mittel (npl)	liquid assets
Folgeanalyse (f)	sequential analysis
Fonds (m)	
Amortisations — , Tilgungs —	sinking fund, amortisation fund
Werbe —	advertising budget/fund
bewilligter —	advertising appropriation
Förderung (f)	
— der Führungskräfte (fpl)	executive advancement
Verkaufs —	sales promotion
Förderwesen (n)	
innerbetriebliches —	materials handling
Formulierung (f)	
— der Unternehmenspolitik (f)	policy formulation
— der Unternehmensstrategie (f)	strategy formulation
Forschung (f)	
— sabteilung (f)	research department
— und Entwicklung (f)	research and development (R & D)
Marketing- —	marketing research
Markt —	market research
Motivations —	motivational research
Produkt —	product research
Schreibtisch —	desk research
System —	systems research
Unternehmens —	operations/operational research (OR)
Verbraucher —	consumer research
Verhaltens —	behavioural science
Werbe —	advertising research
Wirtschafts —	economic research
Fortbildungsangebote (npl)	extension services
fortlaufend	
— e Bestandsaufnahme,	perpetual inventory,

— e Lager(bestands)aufnahme (*f*)	continuous stocktaking
— er Produktionsablauf (*m*)	continuous flow production
Fortschrittskontrolle (*f*)	progress control
führen	to manage, direct
Führer (*m*)	
Markt —	market leader
Preis —	price leader
Führung (*f*)	
— durch Vorgabe (*f*) von Programmen (*npl*)	programmed management
— durch Vorgabe (*f*) von Zielen (*npl*)	management by objectives (MBO)
— sebenen (*fpl*):	
auf nachgeordneten —	down the line
Unternehmensführung (*f*)	multiple management
unter Beteiligung (*f*) nachgeordneter —	
— sfähigkeit(en) (*f(pl)*)	executive competence
— sfunktion (*f*)	managerial function
— sgremium (*n*)	executive board
— skontrolle (*f*)	managerial control
— smethoden (*fpl*), — smethodik (*f*)	management techniques
— snachfolge (*f*), — snachwuchs (*m*)	management succession
— srolle (*f*)	leadership
— sspiel (*n*)	management game
— sstil (*m*)	managerial style
— sstruktur (*f*)	managerial structure, line of command
— steam (*n*)	management team
— stheorie (*f*)	management theory
— sverfahren (*npl*)	management practices
Betriebs —	business management
Wissenschaft (*f*) (von) der —	management science
wissenschaftliche —	scientific management
dynamisches — smodell (*n*)	dynamic management model
Menschen — , Personal —	manpower management
oberstes — sorgan (*n*)	chief executive
Unternehmens —	management, executive
— unter Beteiligung (*f*) nachgeordneter Führungsebenen (*fpl*)	multiple management
Wissenschaft (*f*) (von) der —	management science
Führungskraft (*f*)	manager, executive

— der untersten Ebene (*f*)	first-line manager
Linien —	line manager
Führungskräfte (*fpl*)	executive
— entwicklung (*f*)	executive/management development
— strategie (*f*)	executive manpower strategy
Aufstieg (*m*) der —	executive advancement
Ausbildungsmethode (*f*) für —	managerial grid
(Be-)Förderung (*f*) der —	executive advancement
Vergütung (*f*) der —	executive compensation
Vermittlung, (An-) Werbung (*f*) von — n	executive search
Fundsvermögen (*n*)	asset value
Funktion (*f*)	
Führungs —	managerial function
funktional	
— e Analyse (*f*)	functional analysis
— e Aufteilung (*f*)	functional layout
— e Beziehungen (*fpl*)	functional relations
— e Kostenrechnung (*f*)	functional costing
— es Management (*n*)	functional management
— e Organisation (*f*)	functional organisation
— e Verantwortlichkeiten (*fpl*)	functional responsibility
Fusion (*f*)	amalgamation, merger

G

Gebiet (*n*)	
Absatz — , Handels —	sales area, trading area
Verkaufs —	sales area, sales territory
Wachstums —	growth area
Gefälle (*n*)	
Lohn —	wage differential
Preis —	price differential
gegenwärtig	
— er Nettowert (*m*)	net present value (NPV)
Methode (*f*) des — en Wertes (*m*)	present value method
Gehalt (*m*)	
— sprogressionskurve (*f*)	salary progression curve
— sstruktur (*f*)	salary structure
— sverzeichnis (*n*)	payroll
Vergütung (*f*) neben — oder Lohn (*m*)	fringe benefit
Geheimabsprache (*f*)	collusion
Geltung (*f*)	
Marken —	brand acceptance

Gemeinkosten (*pl*)	overhead expenses
— lohn (*m*)	indirect labour
Aufteilungsverfahren (*n*) für —	overheads recovery
Fabrik —	factory overheads
Verwaltungs —	administrative overheads
gemeinnützig	non-profit making
gemeinsam	
— e Beratung (*f*)	joint consultation
— es Risiko (*n*)	joint venture
— e Sprache (*f*)	common language
— e Verhandlungen (*fpl*)	joint negotiations
— e Vertretung (*f*)	joint representation
Gemeinschaft (*f*)	
— sunternehmen (*n*)	joint venture (company)
an einem — beteiligte Gesellschaften (*fpl*)	joint venture companies
Arbeits —	working party, task force
Interessen —	pooling arrangements, combine
genehmigtes Kapital (*n*)	authorised capital
Generaldirektor (*m*)	general manager, managing director, chief executive
stellvertretender —	deputy managing director
Genossenschaft (*f*)	
Berufs —	trade association
geplant	
— e Instandhaltung (*f*)	planned maintenance
— e Obsoleszenz (*f*), — e Veralterung (*f*)	planned obsolescence
— e Wartung (*f*)	planned maintenance
Gerät (*n*)	
Peripherie — e (*pl*)	peripheral equipment
Gerichtsbarkeit (*f*)	jurisdiction
gesamt	
— e Produktionsanlagen (*fpl*)	production complex
— e Unternehmensziele (*npl*)	overall company objectives
Gesamtziele (*npl*) des Unternehmens (*n*)	overall company objectives
Geschäft (*n*)	
— sbeziehungen (*fpl*)	business relations
— sführender Direktor (*m*)	executive director
nicht — sführender Direktor (*m*)	non-executive director

— sjahr (*n*)	business year, financial year
— sleiter (*m*)	manager
stellvertretender —	assistant manager
— spolitik (*f*)	business policy
— sprognose (*f*)	business forecasting
— sstrategie (*f*)	business strategy
— sumsatz (*m*)	sales turnover
Abwicklung (*f*), Auflösung (*f*) eines — s	winding-up
Hedge- —	hedging operation
Kopplungs —	package deal
Sicherungs —	hedging operation
Gesellschaft (*f*)	
— svermögen (*n*)	net worth, joint capital, social stock
an einem Gemeinschaftsunternehmen (*n*) beteiligte — en (*fpl*)	joint venture companies
Beteiligungs —	affiliate company
Dach — , Holding —	holding company
Mutter —	parent company
nahestehende —	associate company
Tochter —	affiliate company, subsidiary company
Gespräch (*n*)	
Verkaufs —	sales talk
gestaffelter Urlaub (*m*)	staggered holidays
gestalten	to structure
Gestaltung (*f*)	
Arbeits —	work structuring
Produkt —	product design
System —	systems design
Gewerkschaft (*f*)	union, trade union
— spflichtiger Betrieb (*m*)	closed shop
Gewinn (*m*)	profit, pay-off
Kosten-/Umsatz-/— analyse, Kosten-/— -/Volumen- analyse (*f*)	cost, volume, profit analysis
Vertriebskosten- (*pl*) und — aùfschlag (*m*)	mark-up
— aussichten (*fpl*)	profit outlook
— auswirkung (*f*)	profit impact, profit implication
— beteiligung (*f*)	profit sharing
— einbehaltung (*f*)	ploughback
— faktoranalyse (*f*), Analyse (*f*) der — faktoren (*mpl*)	profit factor analysis

gezielte Bemühungen

— leistung (*f*)	profit performance
— marge (*f*)	profit margin
— n (*pl*) halten	to hold margins
— maximierung (*f*)	profit maximisation
— motiv (*n*)	profit motive
— optimierung (*f*)	profit optimisation
— pro Aktie (*f*)	per-share earnings, earnings per share
— projektion (*f*)	profit projection
— -/Umsatzrelation (*f*), -verhältnis (*n*)	profit-volume ratio (P/V)
— schwelle (*f*)	breakeven point
— spanne (*f*)	profit margin, return on sales
— strategie (*f*)	profit strategy
— streben (*n*)	profit motive
— verbesserung (*f*)	profit improvement
— zentrum (*n*)	profit centre
— ziel (*n*)	profit goal, profit target
Brutto —	gross profit
einbehaltener —	retained earnings
Netto — , Rein —	net profit, net margin
thesaurierter —	retained earnings
gezielte Bemühungen (*fpl*) um Produktivitätssteigerung (*f*)	productivity drive
Gitterstruktur (*f*)	grid structure
greifbare Vermögenswerte (*mpl*)	tangible assets
Gremium (*n*)	
Führungs —	executive board
Grenzkosten (*pl*)	marginal cost
— rechnung (*f*)	marginal/direct costing
Grundkapital (*n*)	authorised capital
Grundstückbelastung (*f*)	
Wertverschlechterung (*f*) durch —	dilution of equity
Gruppe (*f*)	
— nanreiz (*m*)	group incentive
— nausbildung (*f*)	group training
— nbonus (*m*)	group bonus
— ndynamik (*f*)	group dynamics, methectics
— training (*n*)	group training
Arbeits —	working party, task force
Produkt —	product group
T- — ntraining (*n*)	T-group training
Güter (*npl*)	
Industrie —	industrial goods

Investitions —   capital goods, industrial
                                      goods
Konsum — , Verbrauchs —   consumer goods
Guthaben (*n*)   assets
sofort einlösbare — (*pl*)   quick assets

H

Halbfertigware(n) (*f*(*pl*))   work in progress
Handel (*m*)
— sgebiet (*n*)   trading area
Börsen — , Effekten —   jobbing
Festlegung (*f*) der — swege   routing
(*mpl*)
Patent —   patent trading
Händler (*m*)
Zwischen — für Software-   software broker
Vertrieb (*m*)
Handlungskosten (*pl*)
allgemeine —   on-cost
Hardware (*f*)   hardware
Häufigkeit (*f*)
— sverteilung (*f*)   frequency distribution
Umschlags — des Kapitals (*n*)   asset turnover
Haupt
— buchhalter (*m*)   chief accountant
— büro (*n*)   head office
— einkäufer (*m*)   chief buyer
Hebelwirkung (*f*)   leverage
Hedge-Geschäft (*n*)   hedging operation
herabsetzen
Preise (*mpl*) —   to cut prices
Herausforderung (*f*) durch die   job challenge
Aufgabe (*f*)
Herkunft (*f*)
Mittel — und -einsatz (*m*)   source and disposition
                                      of funds
Heuristik (*f*)   heuristics
Hierarchie (*f*)
Ziel —   hierarchy of goals
Hilfs —
— lohn (*m*)   indirect labour
Zuteilung (*f*) von — mitteln   allocation of resources
(*npl*)
— operationen (*fpl*)   ancillary operations
horizontale Integration (*f*)   horizontal integration

I

Ideenerzeugung (*f*)
  spontane —   brainstorming
Image (*n*)
  Marken —   brand image
  Produkt —   product image
  Unternehmens —   corporate image
immaterielle Werte (*mpl*)   intangible assets
in Abrechnung (*f*) bringen   to take off
Index (*m*)
  Wachstums —   growth index
indirekt
  — e Ausgaben (*fpl*)   indirect expenses
  — e Kosten (*pl*)   indirect cost(s)
    Aufteilungsverfahren (*n*) recovery of expenses
      für —
Industrie (*f*)
  — dynamik (*f*)   industrial dynamics
  — güter (*npl*)   industrial goods
  — lle Fertigungstechnik (*f*) industrial engineering
  — spionage (*f*)   industrial espionage
  Wachstums —   growth industry
Information (*f*)
  — sbearbeitung (*f*)   information handling
  — sfluß (*m*)   information flow
  — snetz (*n*)   information network
  — ssystem (*n*)   information system
    — auf Computer-Basis (*f*) computerised infor-
                       mation system (COINS)
  — stechnologie (*f*)   information technology
  — stheorie (*f*)   information theory
  — sverarbeitung (*f*)   information processing
  Archivierung (*f*) von — en (*pl*) information retrieval
  Kontroll —   control information
  Management- — en (*pl*)   management informa-
                       tion
  Management- — ssystem (*n*) management infor-
                       mation system (MIS)
  Markt — en (*pl*)   market intelligence
  Raten und Schätzen (*n*) auf- gues(s)timate
    grund bekannter — en (*pl*)
  Wiedergewinnung (*f*) von   information retrieval
    — en (*pl*)
  Wirtschafts —   economic intelligence
informelle Organisation (*f*) informal organisation
Inhalt (*m*),
  Arbeits — , Stellen —   work content
Innenrevision (*f*)   internal audit

innerbetrieblich	
— e Förderwesen (*npl*)	materials handling
— e Tarifverhandlungen (*fpl*)	plant bargaining
— es Training (*n*)	in-plant training
— e Warenverteilung (*f*)	physical distribution management
inoffizieller Streik (*m*)	unofficial strike
Input —	
— -Output-Investitionsportefolioanalyse, — -Output-Analyse (*f*)	input-output analysis
— -Output-Investitionsportefoliotabelle, — -Output-Tabelle (*f*)	input-output table
— -Output-Verhältnis (*n*) des Investitionsportefolios (*n*)	capital-output ratio
Instandhaltung (*f*)	
geplante —	planned maintenance
vorsorgliche —	preventive maintenance
Instanzenzug (*m*)	chain/line of command
Integration (*f*)	
horizontale —	horizontal integration
vertikale —	vertical integration
integriertes Projekt-Management (*n*)	integrated project management (IPM)
intensiv	
— e Produktion (*f*)	intensive production
kapital —	capital intensive
Interdependenz (*f*)	trade-off
Interesse (*n*)	
— an der Arbeit (*f*)	job interest
— ngemeinschaft (*f*)	pooling arrangements
intern	
— e Rechnungsprüfung (*f*)	internal audit
— e Rendite (*f*)	internal rate of return (IRR)
Interview (*n*)	
Tiefen —	depth interview
intuitive Unternehmensführung (*f*)	intuitive management
n Umlauf (*m*) setzen	flotation
nvestition (*f*)	
— sanalyse (*f*)	investment analysis
— sbeurteilung (*f*), — sbewertung (*f*)	capital expenditure appraisal, investment appraisal
— sbudget (*n*)	investment budget
— sgüter (*npl*)	industrial goods, capital goods

— skriterien (*npl*)	investment criteria
— sportefeuille (*n*)	investment mix
— sprogramm (*n*)	investment programme
— srendite (*f*), — srentabilität (*f*)	return on investment
Bewertung (*f*) der — splanung (*f*)	capital project evaluation
Input-Output- — sportefolio-analyse (*f*)	input-output analysis
Input-Output- — sportefolio-tabelle (*f*)	input-output table
Input-Output-Verhältnis (*n*) des — sportefolios (*n*)	capital-output ratio
Output- — sportefolio (*n*)	output budgeting
Ist	
Aufstellung (*f*) des — -Budgets (*n*)	programme budgeting
Soll-/ — -Vergleich (*m*)	performance against objectives

J

Jahr (*n*)	
Finanz — , Geschäfts —	financial year
Rechnungs — , Wirtschafts —	fiscal year, business year
Joint Venture (Gemeinschaftsunternehmen (*n*))	joint venture

K

Kalkulation (*f*)	cost-accounting
— snormen (*fpl*)	cost standards
Kampagne (*f*)	
Produktivitäts —	productivity campaign/drive
Verkaufs —	sales drive
Werbe —	advertising campaign
Kampf (*m*)	
Lohn —	labour conflict, wage dispute
Kapazität (*f*)	
— sauslastung (*f*)	capacity utilisation
Anlagen — , Betriebs —	plant capacity
Fertigungs —, Produktions —	manufacturing capacity
überschüssige —	excess capacity
Kapital (*n*)	
— ausstattung (*f*)	gearing
— beschaffung (*f*)	capital raising
— bildung (*f*)	capital formation

— bindung (*f*)	capital commitment
— budget (*n*)	capital budget
— budgetierung (*f*)	capital budgeting
— intensiv	capital intensive
— isieren	to capitalise
— isiert	
über —	overcapitalised
unter —	undercapitalised
— isierung (*f*)	capitalisation
—-/Produktionsrelation (*f*),	capital-output ratio
—-/Produktionsverhältnis (*n*)	
— rendite (*f*)	return on capital
— ströme (*mpl*)	funds flows
— struktur (*f*)	capital structure
— zuteilung (*f*)	capital rationing
Aktien —	share capital
Anleihe —	loan capital
ausgegebenes —	issued capital
Betriebs —	working/circulating capital
Eigen —	net worth, equity
Rendite (*f*) des — s	return on equity
eingesetztes —	capital employed
Rendite (*f*) des eingesetzten — s	return on capital employed (ROCE)
genehmigtes — , Grund —	authorised capital
mit — ausstatten	to capitalise
Risiko —	venture capital, risk capital
Stamm —	authorised capital
Umschlagshäufigkeit (*f*) des — s	asset turnover
Verwaltung (*f*) von — anlagen (*fpl*)	investment management
Karriereplanung (*f*)	career planning
Kartellabkommen (*n*)	pooling arrangements
Kasse (*f*)	
— nbudget (*n*)	cash budget
— nbudgetierung (*f*)	cash budgeting
— nkennziffer (*f*)	cash ratio
Käufermarkt (*m*)	buyers' market
Kauf (*m*)	
Wahl (*f*) zwischen Eigenfertigung (*f*) und —	make-or-buy decision
Kennzahl (*f*)	
Liquiditäts —	current ratio
Kennziffer (*f*)	
Betriebs —	accounting ratio

Kette

Finanz —	management ratio, financial ratio
Kassen —	cash ratio
Liquiditäts —	liquidity ratio
Kette (f)	
Vertriebs —	chain of distribution
Klassifizierung (f)	
Stellen —	job classification
Klima (n)	
Betriebs —	human relations
Know-how (n)	know-how
Kollegialprinzip (n)	
Management (n) nach dem —	participative management
Kommunikation (f)	
— snetz (n)	communications network
— stheorie (f)	communications theory
— swege (mpl)	channels of communication
Konglomerat (n)	conglomerate
Konjunktur (f)	
— aussichten (fpl),	market prospects
— trend (m), — verlauf (m)	economic trends
— voraussage (f)	business forecasting
— zyklus (m)	business cycle
Konkurrenz (f)	
— analyse (f)	competitor analysis
— fähiger Preis (m), — preis (m)	competitive price
konsolidierte Konten (npl)	consolidated accounts
Konsolidierung (f)	consolidation
Konsortium (n)	consortium, syndicate
Konstruktion (f)	design engineering
technische Abteilung (f) und — sbüro (n)	engineering and design department
— stechnik (f)	design engineering
Konsumentenwünsche (mpl)	
Befriedigung (f) der —	consumer satisfaction
Konsumgüter (npl)	consumer goods
Kontingent (n)	
Absatz — , Verkaufs —	sales quota
Konten (npl)	
konsolidierte —	consolidated accounts
Sammel —	group accounts
Kontrolle (f)	control
— durch Unternehmensleitung (f)	managerial control

adaptive — , Anpassungs —	adaptive control
Aufsichtsrats —	board control
Budget — , Budgetierungs —	budgetary/budgeting control
Fertigungs —	manufacturing/process control
Finanz —	financial control
Fortschritts —	progress control
Kosten —	cost control
Kredit —	credit control
Lagerbestands —	stock/inventory control
numerische —	numerical control
Produktions —	manufacturing control, production control
Produktionsplanung (*f*) und - —	production planning and control
Qualitäts —	quality control (QC)
umfassende —	total quality control
Stapel —	batch control
statistische —	statistical control
Verfahrens —	process control
Verfahren (*n*) zur Verwaltungs —	administrative control procedure
Kontroll —	
— funktion (*f*) des Managements (*n*), der Unternehmensleitung (*f*)	supervisory management
— ieren	to monitor
— ierte Kosten (*pl*)	managed costs
— information (*f*)	control information
— spanne (*f*)	span of control
administrative — verfahren, verwaltungstechnische — verfahren (*npl*)	administrative control procedures
Konzept (*n*)	
Wert —	value concept
Konzeption (*f*)	
Produkt —	product conception
Koppelung (*f*)	
Rück —	feedback
— ssystem (*n*)	closed loop
Kopplungsgeschäft (*n*)	package deal
Körperschaftssteuer (*f*)	corporation tax
Kosten (*pl*)	
— abweichung (*f*)	cost variation
— analyse (*f*)	cost analysis
— aufschlüsselung (*f*)	allocation of costs
— aufteilungsverfahren (*n*)	absorption costing

Kosten

— bewußtsein (*n*)	cost awareness, cost consciousness
— degression (*f*)	economy of scale
— -/Gewinn-/Volumen-analyse, — -/Umsatz-/Gewinnanalyse (*f*)	cost, volume, profit analysis
— -/Nutzenanalyse (*f*)	cost-benefit analysis (CBA)
— faktor (*m*)	cost factor
— progression (*f*)	diseconomy of scale
— schwelle (*f*)	breakeven point
— senkung (*f*)	cost reduction
— spezifikationsverfahren (*n*)	direct costing
— stelle (*f*)	cost centre
— struktur (*f*)	cost structure
— träger (*m*)	profit-centre
— rechnung (*f*)	profit-centre accounting
— umlage (*f*)	allocation of costs
— wirksamkeit (*f*)	cost effectiveness
— zuschlag (*m*)	on-cost, allocation of costs
allgemeine Handlungs —	on-cost
alternative —	opportunity cost
Anlauf —	set-up costs
direkte —	direct costs
durchschnittliche —, Durchschnitts —	average cost
Ermittlung (*f*) der Erzeugnis —	product costing
fixe —	fixed costs
Gemein —	overheads
Aufteilungsverfahren (*n*) für —	recovery of expenses
Grenz —	marginal cost
indirekte —	indirect cost
Aufteilungsverfahren (*n*) für —	recovery of expenses
kontrollierte —	managed costs
laufende Betriebs —	current expenditure
Marginal —	marginal costs
Produktions —	production costs, cost of production
Regie —	on-cost
Soll —	standard cost
sprungfixe —	semi-variable costs
Standard —	standard costs
Stillegungs —	closing-down cost
System — voranschlag (*m*)	estimating systems costs
variable —	variable costs

114

verantwortungsbezogene Erfassung (*f*) von — und Leistungen (*fpl*)	responsibility accounting
Vertriebs —	distribution costs
—- und Gewinnaufschlag (*m*)	mark-up
Verwaltungsgemein —	administrative overheads
Wiederbeschaffungs —	replacement cost
Kostenrechnung (*f*)	cost accounting, costing
— für Serienfertigung (*f*)	process costing
— sart (*f*)	accounting model
funktionale —	functional costing
Grenz —	direct costing, marginal costing
Plan —	standard costing
Produkt —	direct costing, product costing
Standard —	standard costing
variable —	variable costing
Kraft (*f*)	
Ertrags —	earning power
Führungs —	executive
— auf unterster Ebene (*f*)	first-line manager
Kräfte (*fpl*)	
Führungs — entwicklung (*f*)	management/executive development
Ausbildungsmethode (*f*) für Führungs —	managerial grid
Markt —	market forces
Fluktuation (*f*) der Nachwuchs —	trainee turnover
'krank feiern'	*absenteeism
kreativ	
— es Denken (*n*)	creative thinking, brainstorming
— es Marketing (*n*)	creative marketing
Kredit (*m*)	
— aufnahmemöglichkeit (*f*)	borrowing facility
— kontrolle (*f*)	credit control
— verwaltung (*f*)	credit management
ein —, der sich selbst liquidiert	self-liquidating credit
Kreisdiagramm (*n*)	pie chart
Kriterien (*npl*)	
Investitions —	investment criteria
kritisch	
— e Ablaufstufen (*fpl*)	critical path
Analyse (*f*) der — en Ablaufstufen	critical path analysis (CPA)

— e Masse (*f*)	critical mass
— er Pfad (*m*)	critical path
Analyse (*f*) des -en — es (*m*)	critical path analysis (CPA)
Methode (*f*) des — en Pfades (*m*)	critical path method (CPM)
Kunde (*m*)	
— nausrichtung (*f*)	customer orientation
— nbetreuung (*f*)	after-sales service
— ndienst (*m*)	customer service
— nach dem Verkauf (*m*)	after-sales service
— nprofil (*n*)	customer profile
— nwerbung (*f*) durch Sonderangebote (*npl*)	leader merchandising
Kurve (*f*)	
Gehaltsprogressions —	salary progression curve
Lern —	learning curve
kurzfristig	
— e Mittel (*npl*)	quick assets
— e Planung (*f*)	short-term planning
— e Verbindlichkeiten (*fpl*)	current liabilities
Kybernetik (*f*)	cybernetics

L

Lage (*f*)	
Preis —	price range
Lager (*n*)	
— aufnahme, — bestandsaufnahme (*f*)	stocktaking
fortlaufende —	continuous stocktaking, perpetual inventory
— bestandskontrolle (*f*)	inventory control, stock control
— bewertung (*f*)	stock valuation
— haltung (*f*)	warehousing
— umschlag (*m*)	inventory turnover, stock turnover
(Ein-) — ung (*f*)	warehousing
langfristige Planung (*f*)	long range, long term planning
laufend	
— e Ausgaben (*fpl*)	running expenses
— e Betriebsausgaben (*fpl*)	current expenditure
— e Betriebskosten (*pl*)	current expenditure
— e Verbindlichkeiten (*fpl*)	current liabilities
Leasing (*n*)	leasing

Leben (*n*)	
— serwartung (*f*) des/eines	product life expectancy
Produktes (*n*)	
— sfähig	viable
— sfähigkeit (*f*)	viability
— szyklus (*m*) (eines Pro-	life-cycle (of a product)
duktes (*n*))	
wirtschaftliche — sdauer (*f*)	product life
des Produktes (*n*)	
Wirtschafts —	economic life
Lehrgangsleiter (*m*)	training officer
leisten	
Pionierarbeit (*f*) —	to pioneer
Leistung (*f*)	output, production
— in der/einer Stelle (*f*)	job performance
— sbeurteilung (*f*)	performance evaluation, rating
— der Büroangestellten (*pl*)	clerical work measurement (CWM)
— sbewertung (*f*)	performance evaluation, rating
— des Büropersonals (*n*)	clerical work measurement (CWM)
— sbezogene Vergütung (*f*)	payment by results
— seinstufung (*f*)	performance rating, merit rating
— sfähigkeit (*f*)	efficiency
— sgerechte Vergütung (*f*)	payment by results
— smaßstäbe (*mpl*)	performance standards
— smessung (*f*)	performance measurement
— sorientierte Vergütung (*f*)	payment by results
— splanung (*f*)	performance budgeting
— svorgabe (*f*)	performance standards
Ertrags —	earnings performance
Gewinn —	profit performance
Produkt —	product performance
Sozial — en (*pl*)	fringe benefits
verantwortungsbezogene	responsibility
Erfassung (*f*) von Kosten	accounting
(*pl*) und — en (*pl*)	
Vorgabe —	standard performance
zulässiger Zeitraum (*m*),	time-span of discretion
zulässige Zeitspanne (*f*) für	
unterdurchschnittliche —	
eiten	
_eiten	to manage
_eiter (*m*)	manager

Leitung

Betriebs —	plant manager, works manager
Einkaufs —	purchasing manager
Geschäfts —	manager
stellvertretender —	assistant manager
Lehrgangs —	training officer
Marketing- —	marketing manager
Personal —	personnel manager
Produktions —	production manager
Trainings —	training officer
Verkaufs —	sales manager
Vertriebs —	distribution manager
Werbe —	advertising manager
Werks —	works manager, plant manager
Leitung (f)	management
Betriebs —	operating management
Büro —	office management
Personal —	personnel management
Produktions —	production management
Sparten —	divisional management
Stabs —	staff management
Unternehmens —	(top) management
Kontrollfunktion (f) der —	supervisory management
Organogramm (n) der —	management chart
risikobereite —	venture management
Vorgehen (n) der —	top management approach
wirksame —	managerial effectiveness
Verkaufs —	market management, sales management
Leitzahl (f)	benchmark
lenken	to manage
Lenkung (f), Unternehmens —	management
Lern	
— kurve (f)	learning curve
programmierter — prozeß (m)	programmed learning
programmiertes — en (n)	programmed learning
Lieferzeit (f)	lead time
linear	
—e Programmierung (f)	linear programming
— e Verantwortung (f), — e Verantwortlichkeit (f)	linear responsibility
Linie (f)	
— nassistent (m)	line assistant
— nbefugnis (f)	line authority
— nführungskraft (f)	line executive, line manager

118

— n-Management (*n*)	line management
— n-Manager (*m*)	line manager
— norganisation (*f*)	line organisation
— nvollmacht (*f*)	line authority
— und Stab (*m*), Stab und —	line and staff
Liquidation (*f*), Liquidations- verfahren (*n*)	winding-up
liquide Mittel (*npl*)	liquid assets
Verwaltung (*f*) der — n —	cash management
Liquidierung (*f*)	liquidation
Liquidität (*f*)	
— skennzahl (*f*)	current ratio
— skennziffer (*f*)	liquidity ratio
Liste (*f*)	
Lohn —	payroll
Lizenzaustausch (*m*)	cross-licensing
Lockvogelangebot (*n*)	loss leader
Logistik (*f*)	logistics
logistisches Verfahren (*n*)	logistic process
Lohn (*m*)	
— gefälle (*n*)	wage differential
— liste (*f*)	payroll
— struktur (*f*)	wage structure
— verhandlungen (*fpl*) mit Produktivitätsverein- barungen (*fpl*)	productivity bargaining
Fabrikations — , Fer- tigungs —	direct labour
Gemeinkosten —	indirect labour
Hilfs —	indirect labour
Vergütung (*f*) neben Gehalt (*n*) oder —	fringe benefit
ohnen	
sich —	to pay off
Losgröße (*f*)	
Fabrikation (*f*) nach — n (*pl*)	batch production
wirtschaftliche —	economic batch quan- tity, economic order quantity
Lösung (*f*)	
Problem —	problem solving

M

Makler (*m*)	broker
Management (*n*)	management
— by exception	management by excep- tion
— -Dienste (*mpl*)	management services

Manager

— -Information(en) (*f* (*pl*))	management information
— ssystem (*n*)	management information system (MIS)
dynamisches — -Modell (*n*)	dynamic management model
— nach dem Kollegial-prinzip (*n*)	participative management
— -System (*n*)	management system
integriertes —	integrated management system
— -Theorie (*f*)	management theory
allgemeines —	general management
funktionales —	functional management
Kontrollfunktion (*f*) des — s	supervisory management
Linien- —	line management
Matrix- —	matrix management
mittleres —	middle management
operatives —	operations management
Produkt- —	product management
programmiertes —	programmed management
Projekt- —	project management
integriertes —	integrated project management (IPM)
System- —	systems management
wissenschaftliches —	scientific management
Manager (*m*)	manager
Linien- —	line manager
Marken- —	brand manager
Produkt- —	product manager
stellvertretender —	deputy manager
Marge (*f*)	
Brutto —	gross margin
Gewinn —	profit margin
— n halten	to hold margins
Netto —	net margin
marginal	
— analyse (*f*)	marginal analysis
— kosten (*pl*)	marginal cost
Marke (*f*)	brand
— nbetreuer (*m*)	brand manager
— nbewußtsein (*n*)	brand awareness
— nbild (*n*)	brand image
— ngeltung (*f*)	brand acceptance
— nimage (*n*)	brand image
— n-Manager (*m*)	brand manager

— nstrategie (*f*)	brand strategy
— ntreue (*f*)	brand loyalty
Anerkennung (*f*) als	brand recognition
— nartikel (*m*) durch die	
Verbraucher (*mpl*)	
Marketing (*n*)	marketing
→ -Budget (*n*)	marketing budget
— -Forschung (*f*)	marketing research
— -Leiter (*m*)	marketing manager
bewilligte — -Mittel (*npl*)	marketing appropriation
— -Mix (*n*)	marketing mix
— -Strategie (*f*)	marketing strategy
kreatives —	creative marketing
Test- —	test marketing
Markt (*m*)	
— analyse (*f*)	market analysis, survey
— anteil (*m*)	market share
— aufteilung (*f*)	market segmentation
— aussichten (*fpl*)	market prospects
— beurteilung (*f*)	market appraisal
— bewertung (*f*)	market rating
— durchdringung (*f*)	market penetration
— dynamik (*f*)	market dynamics
— einschätzung (*f*)	market rating
— erkundung (*f*)	market exploration
— forschung (*f*)	market research
— führer (*m*)	market leader
— informationen (*fpl*)	market intelligence
— kräfte (*fpl*)	market forces
— möglichkeit (*f*)	market opportunity
— plan (*m*)	market plan
— potential (*n*)	market potential
— preis (*m*)	market price
— profil (*n*)	market profile
— prognose (*f*)	market forecast
— sättigung (*f*), — saturierung (*f*)	market saturation
— segmente (*npl*)	market segments
— segmentierung (*f*)	market segmentation
— struktur (*f*)	market structure
— studie (*f*)	market study
— tendenzen (*fpl*)	market trend
— test (*m*)	market test
— trend (*m*)	market trend
— überblick (*m*)	market survey
— untersuchung (*f*)	market study
— wert (*m*)	market value

aus dem — nehmen	to take off (the market)
Käufer —	buyers' market
Rand —	fringe market
Verkäufer —	sellers' market
Maschine (*f*)	
— nmiete (*f*)	equipment leasing
— nsprache (*f*)	computer language, machine language
Masse (*f*)	
— nproduktion (*f*)	mass production
kritische —	critical mass
Maßnahme (*f*)	
die verschiedenen verkaufs-fördernden — n (*pl*)	promotional mix
Maßstab (*m*)	standard, yardstick
Leistungs — , (Leistungsmaß-stäbe (*pl*))	performance standard(s)
Materialwirtschaft (*f*)	materials handling
materielle Werte (*mpl*)	tangible assets
mathematische Programmierung (*f*)	mathematical programming
Matrix-Management (*n*)	matrix management
Maximierung (*f*)	
Gewinn —	profit maximisation
Media (*npl*)	media
— analyse (*f*)	media analysis
mehrfacher Zugang (*m*)	multi-access
Mehrheitsbeteiligung (*f*)	majority interest
Mehrwertsteuer (*f*)	value added tax (VAT)
Meister (*m*)	foreman
Menge (*f*)	
wirtschaftliche Produktions —	economic manufacturing quantity
Menschenführung (*f*)	manpower management
menschliche Beziehungen (*fpl*) im Betrieb (*m*)	human relations
Merchandising (*n*)	merchandising
Messung (*f*)	
Arbeits —	work measurement
Leistungs —	performance/work measurement
Produktivitäts —	productivity measurement
vorgegebenes System (*n*) zur — von Bewegung und Zeit (*f*)	predetermined motion time system (PMTS)
Methode (*f*)	
— der Arbeitsstichproben (*fpl*)	random observation method

— des gegenwärtigen Wertes (*m*)	present value method
— des kritischen Pfades (*m*)	critical path method (CPM)
— ntechnik (*f*)	methods engineering
— zur Programmbewertung und — überprüfung (*f*)	programme evaluation and review technique (PERT)
Ausbildungs — für Führungskräfte (*fpl*)	managerial grid
Bewertungs — nach Punkten (*mpl*)	points rating method
die verschiedenen Absatz — n (*pl*)	sales mix
Führungs — n (*pl*)	management techniques
Organisation (*f*) und — n (*pl*)	organisation and methods (O & M)
restriktive Arbeits — n (*pl*)	restrictive practices (labour)
Simplex- —	simplex method
Untersuchung (*f*) der — n (*pl*)	methods study
aggressive Verkaufs — n (*pl*)	hard selling
Methodik (*f*)	methods engineering
Führungs —	management techniques
Untersuchung (*f*) der —	methods study
Miete (*f*)	lease, hire, rent
Anlagen —	plant hire
Maschinen —	equipment leasing
Minderheitsbeteiligung (*f*)	minority interest
Mitarbeiter (*mpl*)	
Beförderung (*f*) der —	promotion, personnel promotion
Einführung (*f*) neuer — in das Unternehmen (*n*)	induction
Fehlen (*n*) der —	absenteeism
Versetzung (*f*) der —	staff transfer
vielseitige Verwendbarkeit (*f*) der —	staff mobility
Mitbestimmung (*f*)	industrial democracy, worker participation
mit einer Stelle verbundene Erwartungen (*fpl*)	job expectations
mitlaufend	on-line
Mittel (*npl*)	media, means
— herkunft (*f*) und -einsatz (*m*)	source and disposition of funds
— wert (*m*)	mean
Budget —	budget
bewilligte —	budget appropriation

flüssige —	liquid assets
kurzfristige —	quick assets
liquide —	liquid assets
Verwaltung (*f*) der — n —	cash management
bewilligte Marketing- —	marketing appropriation
Werbe —	advertising media
bewilligte —	advertising appropriation
Wahl (*f*) der —	media selection
Mittler (*m*)	
Werbe —	advertising agent
mittleres Management (*n*)	middle management
Mitwirkung (*f*)	participation
Mix (*n*)	
Marketing- —	marketing mix
Verkaufsförderungs —	promotional mix
Mobilität (*f*)	
— der Arbeitskräfte (*fpl*)	labour mobility
Modalwert (*m*)	mode
Modell (*n*)	model
Buchhaltungs —	accounting model
dynamisches Führungs — , dynamisches Management- —	dynamic management model
Entscheidungs —	decision model
Unternehmens —	corporate model
Möglichkeit (*f*)	
Abschreibungs —	depreciation allowance
Kreditaufnahme — en (*pl*)	borrowing facility
Markt —	market opportunity
morphologische Analyse (*f*)	morphological analysis
Motiv (*n*)	
Gewinn —	profit motive
Motivation (*f*)	
— sfaktor (*m*)	motivator
— sforschung (*f*)	motivational research
Motivierung (*f*)	
Selbst —	self-motivation
multiple Regressionsanalyse (*f*)	multiple regression analysis (MRA)
Muttergesellschaft (*f*)	parent company

N

Nachfassen (*n*)	follow-up
Nachfolge (*f*)	
Führungs —	management succession
Nachfrage (*f*)	demand

— bewertung (*f*)	demand assessment
Befriedigung (*f*) der —	consumer satisfaction
nachgeordnete Führungsebenen (*fpl*)	
auf — n —	down the line
Unternehmensführung (*f*)	multiple management
unter Beteiligung (*f*) — r —	
Nachwuchs (*m*)	trainees
Fluktuation (*f*) der — kräfte (*fpl*)	trainee turnover
Führungs —	management succession
nahestehende Gesellschaft (*f*)	associate company
Nebenoperationen (*fpl*)	ancillary operations
Nebenprodukt (*n*)	by-product
Testen (*n*) des — es	by-product testing
negativer Anreiz (*m*)	disincentive
Netto	
— gewinn (*m*)	net profit
— marge (*f*)	net margin
— umlaufvermögen (*n*)	net current assets
— vermögen (*n*)	net assets
— wert (*m*) des Umlaufvermögens (*n*)	net current assets
gegenwärtiger — wert (*m*)	net present value (NPV)
Netz (*n*)	network
— analyse (*f*)	network analysis
Informations —	information network
Kommunikations —	communications network
Vertriebs —	distribution network
Neubewertung (*f*) des Anlagevermögens (*n*)	revaluation of assets
neutrale Verkaufspolitik (*f*)	soft selling
nicht geschäftsführender Direktor (*m*)	non-executive director
nichtlineare Programmierung (*f*)	non-linear programming
Niederlassung (*f*)	subsidiary company
Niederlegung, Amts — (*f*)	retirement, resignation
Norm (*f*)	standard
Budget —	budget standard
Finanz —	financial standard
Kalkulations —	cost standard
Produktions —	production standard
Zeit —	standard time
Normalabweichung (*f*)	standard deviation
Normalzeit (*f*)	standard time
numerische Kontrolle (*f*)	numerical control
Nutzenanalyse (*f*)	benefit analysis

125

| Kosten-/ — | cost-benefit analysis (CBA) |

O

oberstes Führungsorgan (*n*)	chief executive
Obmann (*m*)	
Betriebs —	shop steward
Obsoleszenz (*f*)	obsolescence
beabsichtigte — , geplante —	planned obsolescence
Öffentlichkeitsarbeit (*f*)	public relations (PR)
offizieller Streik (*m*)	official strike
Ökonom (*m*)	economist
Betriebs —	business economist
Ökonomie (*f*)	
Bewegungs —	motion economy
Operation (*f*)	
— s Research (OR)	operations research (OR)
Hilfs — en, Neben — en (*pl*)	ancillary operations
operativ	
— es Management (*n*)	operations management
— e Planung (*f*)	operational planning
— e Sparte (*f*)	operating division
optimieren	to optimise
Optimierung (*f*)	optimisation
Gewinn —	profit optimisation
Sub —	suboptimisation
Organisation (*f*)	organisation
— splan (*m*)	organisation chart
— splanung (*f*)	organisation planning
— sstruktur (*f*)	organisation structure
— stheorie (*f*)	organisation theory
— und Methoden (*fpl*)	organisation and methods (O & M)
Aufbau (*m*) der — , Entwicklung (*f*) der —	organisational development
funktionale —	functional organisation
informelle —	informal organisation
Linien —	line organisation
Stabs —	staff organisation
Verhalten (*n*) in der —	organisational behaviour
organisatorisch	
— e Änderung (*f*)	organisational change
— e Entwicklung (*f*)	organisational development
— e Wirksamkeit (*f*)	organisational effectiveness

Organogramm (*n*)	organogram, organisation chart
— der Unternehmensführung (*f*), — der Unternehmensleitung (*f*)	management chart
Output (*n*)	
— -Investitionsportefolio (*n*)	output budgeting
Input- — -Analyse (*f*), Input- — -Investitionsportefolioanalyse (*f*)	input-output analysis
Input- — -Investitionsportefoliotabelle (*f*), Input- — -Tabelle (*f*)	input-output table
Input- — -Verhältnis (*n*) des Investitionsportefolios (*n*)	capital-output ratio

P

Paket (*n*)	
Programm —	programme package
Verkaufsförderungs —	promotional mix
Palette (*f*)	
Zusammenfassung (*f*) in — en (*pl*)	palletisation
Panel (*n*)	
Verbraucher —	consumers' panel
parametrische Programmierung (*f*)	parametric programming
Partner (*mpl*)	partners
— schaft (*f*)	partnership
Beziehungen (*fpl*) der Sozial — zueinander	industrial relations
Patenthandel (*m*)	patent trading
Pensionierung (*f*)	retirement
Periode (*f*)	
Bilanzierungs —	accounting period
Peripheriegeräte (*npl*)	peripheral equipment
Personal (*n*)	personnel, staff
— abteilung (*f*)	personnel department
— beratung (*f*)	employee counselling
— beschaffung (*f*)	manpower resourcing
— beurteilung (*f*)	personnel rating
— führung (*f*)	manpower management
— leiter (*m*)	personnel manager
— leitung (*f*)	personnel management
— planung (*f*)	manpower planning
— politik (*f*)	personnel policy

Leistungsbewertung (*f*) des Büro — s	clerical work measurement (CWM)
Prognose (*f*) des — bedarfes (*m*)	manpower forecasting
Überprüfung (*f*), Untersuchung (*f*) des — s	staff inspection
Überprüfung (*f*) des — bestandes (*m*)	manpower audit
vielseitige Verwendbarkeit (*f*) des — s	staff mobility
persönliche Weiterentwicklung (*f*)	personal growth
Pfandbrief (*m*)	debentures
Philosophie (*f*)	
Unternehmens —	company philosophy
Pionier	
— arbeit (*f*) leisten	to pioneer
— produkt(e) (*n*(*pl*))	pioneer product(s)
Plan (*m*)	schedule
— kostenrechnung (*f*)	standard costing
Absatz —	market plan
Aktienbezugsrechts —	stock option plan
Aktions —	action plan
Anreiz —	incentive scheme
Bonus —	bonus scheme
Durchführungs —	action plan
Markt —	market plan
Organisations —	organisation chart
Prämien —	bonus scheme
Produktions —	production schedule
Produktionsanteils — , Anteil (*m*) am Produktions —	share of production plan
taktischer —	tactical plan
Planung (*f*)	scheduling, planning
— sabteilung (*f*)	planning department
— s-, Programmierungs- (und) Budgetierungssystem (*n*)	planning-programming-budgeting system (PPBS)
Absatz —	sales planning
Abteils —	departmental planning
Betriebs —	operational planning
Finanz —	financial planning
Gewinn —	profit planning
Bewertung (*f*) der Investitions —	capital project evaluation
Karriere —	career planning
kurzfristige —	short-term planning
langfristige —	long range, long term planning

operative —	operational planning
Organisations —	organisation planning
Personal —	manpower planning
Produkt —	product planning
Produktions —	production planning
— und -kontrolle (*f*)	production planning and control
Projekt —	project planning
strategische —	strategic planning
System —	systems planning
Umsatz —	sales planning
Unternehmens —	company planning, corporate planning
Vertriebs —	distribution planning
Vorwärts —	forward planning
Zeit —	scheduling
Politik (*f*)	policy
Absatz —	sales policy
Dividenden —	dividend(s) policy
Geschäfts —	business policy
Investitions —	investment policy
Personal —	personnel policy
Preis —	pricing policy
Umsatz —	sales policy
Unternehmens —	company policy
Bekanntgabe (*f*) der —	policy statement
Durchführung (*f*) der —	policy execution
Formulierung (*f*) der —	policy formulation
Verkaufs —	selling policy
aggressive —	hard selling
neutrale —	soft selling
Verkaufsförderungs —	promotional policy
Vertriebs —	distribution policy
Portefeuille (*n*)	
— auswahl (*f*)	portfolio selection
— verwaltung (*f*)	portfolio management
Investitions —	investment mix
Portefolio (*n*)	
Investitions —	
Input-Output- — analyse (*f*)	input-output analysis
Input-Output- — tabelle (*f*)	input-output table
Input-Output-Verhältnis (*n*) des — s	capital-output ratio
Output- —	output budgeting
Position (*f*)	
Wettbewerbs —	competitive position
Postversandwerbung (*f*)	direct mail

Potential

Potential (*n*)
  Entwicklungs —   development potential
  Führungskräfte —   management potential
  Markt —   market potential
  Umsatz — , Verkaufs — sales potential
  Wachstums —   growth potential
potentieller Käufer (*m*)   potential buyer
Prämie (*f*)   premium, bonus
  — nplan (*m*)   bonus scheme
Präsident (*m*)   president
  Vize —   vice president
Preis (*m*)
  — bindung (*f*) der zweiten resale price maintenance
    Hand (*f*)   (RPM)
  — e (*pl*) herabsetzen, — e to cut prices
    senken
  — festsetzung (*f*)   price fixing, price
                        determination
  — führer (*m*)   price leader
  — gefälle (*n*)   price differential
  — lage (*f*)   price range
  — politik (*f*)   pricing policy
  — skala (*f*)   price range
  — strategie (*f*)   pricing strategy
  — struktur (*f*)   price structure
  — unterbietung (*f*)   price cutting
  — unterschied (*m*)   price differential
  Aktien — /Ertragsrelation (*f*), price-earnings ratio
    Aktien — /Ertragsverhältnis (P/E)
    (*n*)
  Festlegung (*f*) der Ver-   transfer pricing
    rechnungs — e (*pl*)
  Konkurrenz — , konkur-   competitive price
    renzfähiger —
  Markt —   market price
  sich gegenseitig verstärkender price escalation
    — auftrieb (*m*)
  zum Selbstkosten —   self liquidating
Primärerhebung (*f*)   field research
Problem (*n*)
  — analyse (*f*)   problem analysis
  — bereich (*m*)   problem area
  — lösung (*f*)   problem solving
  experimentelle Anwendung (*f*) human engineering
    psychologischer Erkenntnisse
    (*fpl*) auf menschliche — e
    (*pl*) im Betrieb (*m*)

Produkt (*n*)

— ablehnung (*f*) durch den Verbraucher (*m*)	consumer resistance
— analyse (*f*)	product analysis
— annahme (*f*) durch den Verbraucher (*m*)	consumer acceptance
— bereich (*m*)	product area/range
— differenzierung (*f*)	product differentiation
— diversifizierung (*f*)	product diversification
— dynamik (*f*)	product dynamics
— entwicklung (*f*)	product development
— erzeugung (*f*)	product generation
— forschung (*f*)	product research
— gestaltung (*f*)	product design
— gruppe (*f*)	product group
— image (*n*)	product image
— konzeption (*f*)	product conception
— kostenrechnung (*f*)	product costing, direct costing
— leistung (*f*)	product performance
— -Management (*n*)	product management
— -Manager (*m*)	product manager
— planung (*f*)	product planning
— profil (*n*)	product profile
— programm (*n*)	product line
— rentabilität (*f*)	product profitability
— skala (*f*)	product range
— sortiment (*n*)	product mix
— strategie (*f*)	product strategy
— test (*m*), — testen (*n*)	product testing
— verbesserung (*f*)	product improvement
— werbung (*f*)	product advertising
Entwicklung (*f*) neuer — e (*pl*)	new product development
Lebenserwartung (*f*) eines — es	product life expectancy
Lebenszyklus (*m*) eines — es	life cycle of a product
Neben —	by-product
Testen (*n*) des — es	by-product testing
Pionier —	pioneer product
Rentabilität (*f*) des — es	product profitability
Streichung (*f*) von — en (*pl*), eines — es	product abandonment
verlustbringendes —	loss maker
wirtschaftliche Lebensdauer (*f*) eines — es	product life

Produktion (*f*) production, output

— santeilsplan (*m*)	share of production
— sbreite (*f*)	product diversification
— sfluß (*m*)	flow line
— skapazität (*f*)	manufacturing capacity
— skontrolle (*f*)	manufacturing/production control
— skosten (*pl*)	production costs, cost of production
— sleiter (*m*)	production manager
— sleitung (*f*)	production management
— nach dem Baukastenprinzip (*n*)	modular production
— snorm(en) (*f* (*pl*))	production standard(s)
— splan (*m*)	production plan, production schedule
Anteil (*m*) am —	share of production plan
— splanung (*f*)	production planning, scheduling
— und -kontrolle (*f*)	production planning and control
— sprogramm (*n*)	product line
— sprozeß (*m*)	production process
— stechnik (*f*)	production engineering
— sziele (*npl*)	production targets
Budgetierung (*f*) im — sbereich (*m*)	output budgeting
Fließband —	line production
fortlaufender — sablauf (*m*)	continuous flow production
gesamte — sanlagen (*fpl*)	production complex
intensive —	intensive production
Kapital-/ — srelation (*f*)	capital-output ratio
Kapital-/ — sverhältnis (*n*)	capital-output ratio
Massen —	mass production, flow production
Test —	pilot production
Versuchs —	pilot production
wirtschaftliche — smenge (*f*)	economic manufacturing quantity
Produktivität (*f*)	productivity
— skampagne (*f*)	productivity campaign
— smessung (*f*)	productivity measurement
— svereinbarung (*f*)	productivity agreement
Lohnverhandlungen (*fpl*) mit —	productivity bargaining
— sverhandlung (*f*)	productivity bargaining

Abkommen (*n*) über — sstei-gerungen (*fpl*)	productivity agreement
gezielte Bemühungen (*fpl*) um — ssteigerung (*f*)	productivity drive
•rofessionell	
Erlangung (*f*) eines — en Status (*m*)	professionalisation
•rofil (*n*)	profile
Akquisitions —	acquisition profile
Kunden —	customer profile
Markt —	market profile
Produkt —	product profile
Qualifikations —	personnel specification
Risiko —	risk profile
Unternehmens —	company profile
•rognose (*f*)	forecast
— des Personalbedarfs (*m*)	manpower forecasting
— der technologischen Entwicklung (*f*)	technological forecast
Budget —	budget forecasting
Geschäfts —	business forecasting
Markt —	market forecast
Umsatz —	sales forecast
Wirtschafts —	environmental fore-casting
•rogramm (*n*)	programme schedule
— budgetierung (*f*)	programme budgeting
— paket (*n*)	programme package
Entwicklungs —	development pro-gramme
Führung (*f*) durch Vorgabe (*f*) von — en (*pl*)	programmed manage-ment
Investitions —	investment programme
Methode (*f*) zur — bewertung (*f*) und -überprüfung (*f*)	programme evaluation and review technique (PERT)
Produkt — , Produktions —	product line
Verkaufs —	sales mix
rogrammiert	
— es Lernen (*n*), — er Lernprozeß (*m*)	programmed learning
— es Management (*n*)	programmed manage-ment
•rogrammierung (*f*)	programming, computer programming
— des Computers (*m*), Computer- —	computer programming
dynamische —	dynamic programming

Progression

lineare —	linear programming
mathematische —	mathematical programming
nichtlineare —	non-linear programming
parametrische —	parametric programming
Planungs-, — s- (und) Budgetierungssystem (*n*)	planning-programming-budgeting system (PPBS)
wissenschaftliche —	scientific programming
Progression (*f*)	
Gehalts — skurve (*f*)	salary progression curve
Kosten —	diseconomy of scale
Projekt (*n*)	project
— analyse (*f*)	project analysis
— bewertung (*f*)	project assessment
— -Management (*n*)	project management
integriertes —	integrated project management (IPM)
— planung (*f*)	project planning
Projektion (*f*)	
Gewinn —	profit projection
Prozeß (*m*)	
Entscheidungs —	decision process
Produktions —	production process
Prüfer (*m*)	
Bilanz —	comptroller
Rechnungs —	auditor, comptroller
Prüfung (*f*)	
Betriebs —	operations audit
Betriebsrechnungs —	management audit
Bilanz —	audit, balance sheet auditing
Rechnungs —	audit
interne —	internal audit
Über — des Personalbestandes (*m*)	manpower audit
Psychologie (*f*)	
Betriebs —	industrial psychology
Punkt (*m*)	
— ediagramm (*n*)	scatter diagram
Beurteilungsverfahren (*n*) nach — en (*pl*), Bewertungsmethode (*f*) nach — en (*pl*)	points rating method

Q

Qualifikationen (*fpl*)	
Stellen —	job competence

Qualifikationsprofil (*n*)	personnel specification
Qualität (*f*)	
— skontrolle (*f*)	quality control (QC)
umfassende —	total quality control

R

Randmarkt (*m*)	fringe market
Rat (*m*)	
Aufsichts —	board of directors, executive board
wissenschaftlicher Bei —	brains trust
Betriebs —	works council
Experten —	brains trust
Raten (*n*) und Schätzen (*n*) aufgrund bekannter Informationen (*fpl*)	gues(s)timate
Rationalisierung (*f*)	rationalisation, cost reduction
Raum (*m*)	
Sitzungs —	board room
Reaktion (*f*)	
antizipative —	anticipating response
antizipatorische —	anticipatory response
verspätete —	lag response
Realzeit (*f*)	real time
Rechen —	
— schaftspflicht (*f*)	accountability
— zentrum (*n*)	computer centre
Rechner (*m*)	
Analog —	analogue computer
Digital —	digital computer
Rechnung (*f*)	
— en (*pl*) überprüfen	to audit
— sabschnitt (*m*)	accounting period
— sabteilung (*f*)	accounting department
— sjahr (*n*)	financial year, fiscal year
— sprüfer (*m*)	auditor, comptroller
— sprüfung (*f*)	audit
Betriebs —	management audit
interne —	internal audit
Betriebs — swesen (*n*)	management accounting
Kosten —	cost accounting, costing
— für Serienfertigung (*f*)	process costing
— sart (*f*)	accounting model
funktionale —	functional costing
Grenz —	marginal costing
Plan —	standard costing

Produkt —	product costing
Standard —	standard costing
variable —	variable costing
Kostenträger —	profit centre accounting
Refa-Studie (*f*)	time and motion study, time and methods study
Regressionsanalyse (*f*)	regression analysis
multiple —	multiple regression analysis (MRA)
Relation (*f*)	
Aktienpreis (*m*)/Ertrags —	price-earnings ratio (P/E)
Gewinn-/Umsatz —	profit-volume ratio (P/V)
Kapital- (*n*)/Produktions —	capital-output ratio
Rendite (*f*)	rate of return
— des Eigenkapitals (*n*)	return on equity
— des eingesetzten Kapitals (*n*)	return on capital employed (ROCE)
interne —	internal rate of return (IRR)
Investitions —	return on investment
Kapital —	return on capital
Umsatz —	return on sales
Rentabilität (*f*)	profitability, pay-off
— des Produktes (*n*)	product profitability
— sanalyse (*f*)	profitability analysis
— sschwelle (*f*)	breakeven point
Analyse (*f*) der —	breakeven analysis
Investitions —	return on investment
Produkt —	product profitability
rentieren	
sich —	to pay off
Reorganisation (*f*)	reorganisation
Ressourcen (*pl*)	
Allokation (*f*) der —	resource allocation
Bewertung (*f*) von —	resource appraisal
restriktive Arbeitsmethoden (*fpl*), restriktive Arbeitsverfahren (*npl*)	restrictive practices (labour)
Revision (*f*)	
— durchführen	to audit
Betriebs —	operations audit
Innen —	internal audit
Revisor (*m*)	comptroller
Richtzahl (*f*)	benchmark
Risiko (*n*)	
— analyse (*f*)	risk analysis

— bereite Unternehmens-führung (*f*), Unternehmensleitung (*f*)	venture management
— bewertung (*f*), — einschätzung (*f*)	risk assessment
— kapital (*n*)	venture capital, risk capital
— profil (*n*)	risk profile
gemeinsames —	joint venture
Risiken (*npl*)	
Rücklage (*f*) für unvorhergesehene —	contingency reserve
Rolle (*f*)	
— nrepertoire eines einzelnen	*role set
— nspiel (*n*)	role playing
Führungs —	leadership
Routine (*f*)	routine
Rückkoppelung (*f*)	feedback
— ssystem (*n*)	closed loop
Rücklage (*f*) für unvorhergesehene Risiken (*npl*)	contingency reserve
Rücktritt (*m*)	retirement

S

Sammelkonten (*npl*)	group accounts
Sammlung (*f*)	
Daten —	data gathering
Sanierung (*f*) des Unternehmens (*n*)	company reconstruction
Sättigung (*f*), Saturierung (*f*)	
Markt —	market saturation
Schachtelaufsichtsrat (*m*)	interlocking directorate
Schätzen (*n*)	
Raten (*n*) und — aufgrund bekannter Informationen (*fpl*)	gues(s)timate
Schätzung (*f*)	
Umsatz — , Verkaufs —	sales estimate
Schaufensterdekoration (*f*)	window-dressing
Schiedsverfahren (*n*)	arbitration
Schlichtung (*f*)	conciliation
— sverfahren (*n*)	arbitration
Schreibtischforschung (*f*)	desk research
Schuldner (*mpl*)	debtors
Schulung (*f*)	
zusätzliche —	booster training

Schwelle (*f*)

Ertrags — , Gewinn — , Kosten — , Rentabilitäts —	breakeven point
Analyse (*f*) der Rentabilitäts —	breakeven analysis

Segment (*n*)

Markt — e (*pl*)	market segments
Markt — ierung (*f*)	market segmentation

Sekundärnutzen (*m*)	spin-off effects

Selbst

— einschätzung (*f*)	self appraisal, self assessment
— finanzierung (*f*)	self financing
— motivierung (*f*)	self motivation
zum — kostenpreis (*m*)	self liquidating

senken

Preise (*mpl*) —	to cut prices

Senkung (*f*)

Kosten —	cost reduction
sensibilisieren	to sensitise

Sensitivität (*f*)

— sanalyse (*f*)	sensitivity analysis
— straining (*n*)	sensitivity training
sequentielle Analyse (*f*)	sequential analysis

Serienfertigung (*f*)

Kostenrechnung (*f*) für —	process costing

Serie (*f*)

Zeit —	time series

Setzung (*f*)

Ziel —	goal setting, objective
sich automatisch abdeckend	self liquidating
sich gegenseitig verstärkender Preisauftrieb (*m*)	price escalation
sich bezahlt machen, sich lohnen, sich rentieren	to pay off
sicherer Arbeitsplatz (*m*)	job security

Sicherheit (*f*)

— sbank (*f*)	safety bank
— sbevorratung (*f*)	buffer stock, safety stock
Betriebs —	industrial security

Sicherungsgeschäft (*n*)	hedging operation(s)
Simplex-Methode (*f*)	simplex method
Simulation (*f*)	simulation
Computer- —	computer simulation
simulieren	to simulate
simultane Verarbeitung (*f*)	on-line
Sitzstreik (*m*)	sit-down strike

Skala (*f*)

Preis —	price range

Produkt —	product range
sofort einlösbare Guthaben (*npl*)	quick assets
Software (*f*)	software
Firma für —	software firm
Zwischenhändler (*m*) für — - Vertrieb (*m*)	software broker
Soll (*n*)	
— -/Ist-Vergleich (*m*)	performance against objectives
— kosten (*pl*)	standard costs
Sonderangebot (*n*)	
Kundenwerbung (*f*) durch — e (*pl*)	switch selling, leader merchandising
Sortiment (*n*)	
Beschränkung (*f*) des — s	variety reduction
Produkt — , Waren —	product mix
Sozial —	
— leistungen (*fpl*)	fringe benefits
Beziehungen (*fpl*) der — partner (*mpl*) zueinander	industrial relations
Spanne (*f*)	
Gewinn —	profit margin, return on sales
Kontroll —	span of control
Sparte (*f*)	
— nleitung (*f*)	divisional management
operative —	operating division
Speicherung (*f*) auf/im Computer - (*m*)	computer storage
Spiel (*n*)	
— theorie (*f*)	game theory
Führungs —	management game
Rollen —	role playing
Unternehmens —	business game, management game
Spionage (*f*)	
Industrie —	industrial espionage
spontane Ideenerzeugung (*f*)	brain storming
Sprache (*f*)	
Computer- —	computer language
gemeinsame —	common language
Maschinen —	machine language, computer language
sprungfixe Kosten (*pl*)	semi-variable costs
Stab (*m*)	
— sassistent (*m*)	staff assistant
— sleitung (*f*)	staff management
— sorganisation (*f*)	staff organisation

Linie (*f*) und —	line and staff
Stamm (*m*)	
— baum (*m*)	family tree
— kapital (*n*)	authorised capital
Standard (*m*)	standard
— abweichung (*f*)	standard deviation
— code (*m*)	common language
— isierung (*f*)	standardisation, variety reduction
— kosten (*pl*)	standard cost
— kostenrechnung (*f*)	standard costing
— zeit (*f*)	standard time
Standort (*m*) des Betriebes (*m*)	plant location
Stapel (*m*)	
— kontrolle (*f*)	batch control
— verarbeitung (*f*)	batch processing
statistische Kontrolle (*f*)	statistical control
Status (*m*)	
Erlangung (*f*) eines professionellen —	professionalisation
Steigerung (*f*)	
Produktivitäts —	
Abkommen (*n*) über — en (*pl*)	productivity agreement
gezielte Bemühungen (*fpl*) um —	productivity drive
Bemühungen (*fpl*) um Verkaufs — en (*pl*)	sales expansion effort
Stelle (*f*)	
— nanalyse (*f*)	job analysis
— nanforderung (*f*)	job challenge, job specification
— nanhebung (*f*)	job improvement
— nbeschreibung (*f*)	job description
— nbeurteilung (*f*), — bewertung (*f*)	job evaluation
— nentwurf (*m*)	job design
— nerweiterung (*f*)	job enlargement
— ninhalt (*m*)	work content
Aufgliederung (*f*) des — s	operations breakdown
— nklassifizierung (*f*)	job classification
— nqualifikationen (*fpl*)	job competence
— nvereinfachung (*f*)	job simplification
Befriedigung (*f*) durch die —	job satisfaction
Bereicherung (*f*) durch die —	job enrichment
Interesse (*n*) an der —	job interest
Kosten —	cost centre
Leistung (*f*) in einer/der —	job performance

mit einer — verbundene Erwartungen (*pl*)	job expectations
Zweig —	branch office
̶tellung (*f*)	
Wettbewerbs —	competitive position
̶ellvertretend	
— er Direktor (*m*)	deputy manager, assistant manager
— er Generaldirektor (*m*)	deputy managing director
— er Geschäftsleiter (*m*)	assistant manager
— er Manager (*m*)	deputy manager
— er Vorsitzender (*m*)	vice-chairman, deputy chairman
̶euer (*f*)	tax
— erleichterung (*f*) bei Doppelbesteuerung (*f*)	double taxation relief
Körperschafts —	corporation tax
Mehrwert —	value added tax (VAT)
̶ichprobe (*f*)	
— nentnahme (*f*)	random sampling
Arbeits — n (*fpl*)	activity sampling
Methode (*f*) der — (*fpl*)	random observation method
̶il (*m*)	
Führungs —	managerial style
̶illegen	to shut down
̶illegungskosten (*pl*)	closing down cost
̶raffen	to streamline
̶rategie (*f*)	strategy
Benutzer —	user strategy
defensive —	defensive strategy
Diversifikations — , Diversifizierungs —	diversification strategy
Durchführung (*f*) der —	strategy implementation
Expansions —	expansion strategy
Finanz —	financial strategy
Führungskräfte —	executive manpower strategy
Geschäfts —	business strategy
Gewinn —	profit strategy
Marken —	brand strategy
Marketing- —	marketing strategy
Preis —	pricing strategy
Produkt —	product strategy
Überlebens —	survival strategy
Unternehmens —	corporate strategy
Formulierung (*f*) der —	strategy formulation

strategisch

Verbraucher —	user strategy
Verhandlungs —	negotiation strategy
Wachstums —	growth strategy, expansion strategy
Wettbewerbs —	competitive strategy

strategisch

— e Planung (*f*)	strategic planning
— e Wechselbeziehung (*f*)	strategic interdependence

Streben (*n*)

Gewinn —	profit motive

Streichung (*f*) von Produkten (*pl*), eines Produktes (*n*) — product abandonment

Streik (*m*) — strike

— posten (*m*)	picket
Bummel —	go-slow, work-to-rule
inoffizieller —	unofficial strike
offizieller —	official strike
Sitz —	sit down strike
Sympathie —	walkout
wilder —	wildcat strike

Streubild, Streudiagramm (*n*) — scatter diagram

Ströme (*mpl*)

Kapital —	funds flows

Struktur (*f*) — structure

Autoritäts —	authority structure
Befugnis —	line of command, authority structure
Führungs —	managerial structure
Gehalts —	salary structure
Gitter —	grid structure
Kapital —	capital structure
Kosten —	cost structure
Lohn —	wage structure
Markt —	market structure
Organisations —	organisation structure
Preis —	price structure
Unternehmens —	corporate structure

Stückarbeit (*f*) — piecework

Studie (*f*)

Arbeitsablauf — (n) (*pl*)	work measurement
Arbeits —	work study
Betriebs —	industrial engineering
Bewegungs —	motion study
Durchführbarkeits —	feasibility study
Fall —	case study
Markt —	market study
Refa-, Zeit- und Bewegungs —	time and methods/time and motion study

Suboptimierung (*f*)	suboptimisation
Substanzwert (*m*)	asset value
Sympathiestreik (*m*)	walkout
Syndikat (*n*)	syndicate
Synergie (*f*)	synergy
System (*n*)	system
— analyse (*f*)	systems analysis
— atisch darstellen	to systematise
— atischer Arbeitsplatz-wechsel (*m*)	job rotation
— e und Verfahren (*npl*)	systems and procedures
— entwicklung (*f*), — gestalt-ung (*f*)	systems design
— kostenvoranschlag (*m*)	estimating systems costs
— -Management (*n*)	systems management
— planung (*f*)	systems planning
— technik (*f*)	systems engineering
— theorie (*f*)	systems theory
— verfahren (*n*)	systems approach
— verwaltung (*f*)	systems management
— vorgehen (*n*)	systems approach
an ein — angeschlossen, mitlaufend	on-line
Informations —	informations system
— auf Computer-Basis (*f*)	computerised informa-tion system (COINS)
Management- —	management infor-mation system (MIS)
Management- —	management system
integriertes —	integrated management system
nach — (en) (*pl*) geführtes Unternehmen	system managed company
Planungs-, Programmierungs- und Budgetierungs —	planning-programming-budgeting system (PPBS)
Rückkoppelungs —	closed loop
vorgegebenes — zur Messung (*f*) von Bewegung (*f*) und Zeit (*f*)	predetermined motion time system (PMTS)

T

Tabelle (*f*)	
Input-Output- —, Input-Output-Investitionsporte-folio —	input-output table
Taktik (*f*)	
Wettbewerbs —	competitive tactics
aktischer Plan (*m*)	tactical plan

Tarif (*m*)	
— verhandlungen (*fpl*)	collective bargaining
innerbetriebliche —	plant bargaining
— vertrag (*m*)	collective bargaining agreement
Tätigkeit (*f*)	
— eines Zulieferanten (*m*)	subcontracting
— sdiagramm (*n*)	activity chart
Team (*n*)	
Führungs —	management team
Technik (*f*)	
industrielle Fertigungs —	industrial engineering
Konstruktions —	design engineering
Methoden —	methods engineering
Produktions —	production engineering
System —	systems engineering
Wert —	value engineering
technische Abteilung (*f*) und	engineering and design
Konstruktionsbüro (*n*)	department
Technologie (*f*)	
Informations —	information technology
technologisch	
Prognose (*f*) der — en	technological
Entwicklung (*f*)	forecast(ing)
Teil (*m, n*)	
Ausbildung (*f*) in — analysen (*fpl*)	part analysis training
— haber (*m*)	partner
Training (*n*) durch — nahme (*f*) an externen Seminaren (*npl*)	off-the-job training
Tendenz (*f*)	
Markt — en (*pl*)	market trend
Wirtschafts — en (*pl*)	economic trend
Terminal (*n*)	terminal
Test (*m*)	
— -Marketing (*n*)	test marketing
— produktion (*f*)	pilot production
Eignungs —	aptitude test
Feld- — s (*pl*)	field testing
Markt —	market test
Produkt —	product testing
testen	to debug
Testen (*n*)	
— des Nebenproduktes (*n*)	by-product testing
Produkt —	product testing
T-Gruppentraining (*n*)	T-group training
Thema (*n*)	
Werbe —	advertising theme

Theorie (*f*)	
Entscheidungs —	decision theory
Informations —	information theory
Kommunikations —	communications theory
Management- —	management theory
Organisations —	organisation theory
Spiel —	game theory
System —	systems theory
Verwaltungs —	administrative theory
Wahrscheinlichkeits —	probability theory
Warteschlangen —	queuing theory
thesaurierter Gewinn (*m*)	retained earnings
Tiefe (*f*)	
— nanalyse (*f*)	depth analysis
— ninterview (*n*)	depth interview
Tilgungsfonds (*m*)	sinking fund
Time-Sharing (*n*) (Datenfernübertragung)	time-sharing
Tochtergesellschaft (*f*)	affiliate company, subsidiary company
Training (*n*)	training
— am Arbeitsplatz (*m*)	on-the-job training
— durch Teilnahme (*f*) an externen Seminaren (*npl*)	off-the-job training
— im Betrieb (*m*)	in-plant training
— sleiter (*m*)	training officer
Gruppen —	group training
innerbetriebliches —	in-plant training
Sensitivitäts —	sensitivity training
T-Gruppen —	T-group training
zusätzliches —	booster training
Transportwesen (*n*)	materials handling
Trend (*m*)	trend
exponentieller —	exponential trends
Konjunktur —	economic trend
Markt —	market trend
Treue (*f*)	loyalty
Marken —	brand loyalty

U

Überblick (*m*)	
Markt —	market survey
überflüssige Arbeitsplätze (*fpl*)	redundancy
überkapitalisiert	overcapitalised
Überlebensstrategie (*f*)	survival strategy
Übernahme (*f*)	takeover
— angebot (*n*)	takeover bid

überprüfen	to debug
Rechnungen (*fpl*) —	to audit
Überprüfung (*f*)	
— nach der Ausführung (*f*)	follow-up
— im Feld (*n*)	field testing
— der Finanzlage (*f*)	financial review
— des Personals (*n*)	staff inspection
— des Personalbestands (*m*)	manpower audit
Finanz —	financial review
überschüssige Kapazität (*f*)	excess capacity
Übertragung (*f*)	
Datenfern —	time-sharing
überwachen	to monitor
umfassende Qualitätskontrolle (*f*)	total quality control
Umgruppierung (*f*) der Arbeitskräfte (*fpl*)	redeployment
Umlage (*f*)	
Kosten —	allocation of costs
Umlauf (*m*)	
— vermögen (*n*)	current assets
Netto — ,.Nettowert (*m*) des — s	net current assets
in — setzen	*flotation
Umsatz (*m*)	
— analyse (*f*)	sales analysis
— erwartungen (*fpl*)	sales expectations
— planung (*f*)	sales planning
— politik (*f*)	sales policy
— potential (*n*)	sales potential
— prognose (*f*)	sales forecast
— rendite (*f*)	return on sales
— schätzung (*f*)	sales estimate
— volumen (*n*)	sales volume
— ziel (*n*)	sales goal
Geschäfts —	sales turnover
Gewinn-/ — relation (*f*), -verhaltnis (*n*)	profit-volume ratio (P/V)
Kosten-/ — -/Gewinnanalyse (*f*)	cost, volume, profit analysis
Umschlag (*m*)	
— shäufigkeit (*f*) des Kapitals (*n*)	asset turnover
Lager —	inventory turnover, stock turnover
Umschulung (*f*)	retraining
umstellen auf Computer (*m*)	to computerise
Umstellung (*f*) auf Container (*m*)	containerisation
Umstrukturierung (*f*)	restructuring

Umwelt (f)	environment
unmittelbar geleistete Arbeits- zeit (f)	direct labour
Unterbietung (f)	
Preis —	price cutting
unterkapitalisiert	undercapitalised
Unternehmen (n)	company, firm, enter- prise, concern
— sberater (m)	(management) con- sultant
— sforschung (f)	operational/operations research (OR)
— sführung (f)	management
— unter Beteiligung (f) nachgeordneter Führungs- ebenen (fpl)	multiple management
intuitive —	intuitive management
Organogramm (n) der —	management chart
risikobereite —	venture management
wirksame —	effective management, managerial effectiveness
Wissenschaft (f) (von) der —	management science
— simage (n)	corporate image
— sleitung (f)	management, top management
Kontrolle (f) durch —	managerial control
Kontrollfunktion (f) der —	supervisory manage- ment
Organogramm (n) der —	management chart
risikobereite —	venture management
Vorgehen (n) der —	top management approach
wirksame —	effective management, managerial effectiveness
— smodell (n)	corporate model
— sphilosophie (f)	company philosophy
— splanung (f)	company planning, corporate planning
— spolitik (f)	company policy
Bekanntgabe (f) der —	policy statement
Durchführung (f) der —	policy execution
Formulierung (f) der —	policy formulation
— sprofil (n)	company profile
— sspiel (n)	business game
— sstrategie (f)	corporate strategy
Formulierung (f) der —	strategy formulation
— sstruktur (f)	corporate structure
— swachstum (n)	corporate growth

— swerbung (f)	corporate advertising
— sziel (n)	company goal
— e (pl)	company objectives
gesamte — e (pl)	overall company objectives
Beratungs —	(management) consultancy
*dem — nicht unmittelbar zugehöriger Direktor (m)	outside director
Einführung (f) neuer Mitarbeiter (mpl) in das —	induction
Gemeinschafts —	joint venture
an einem — beteiligte Gesellschaften (fpl)	joint venture companies
Gesamtziele (npl) des — s	overall company objectives
nach System (n) geführtes —	system managed company
Sanierung (f) des — s, Wiederaufbau (m) des — s	company reconstruction
unternehmerische Einstellung (f)	entrepreneurial spirit
Unterprogramm (n) (EDV)	routine
Unterrichtung (f)	briefing
Unterschied (m)	
Preis —	price differential
unterschwellige Werbung (f)	subliminal advertising
Unterstützung (f)	support activity
Untersuchung (f)	
— der Betriebsanlagen (fpl)	plant layout study
— der Methoden (fpl), der Methodik (f)	methods study
— des Personals (n)	staff inspection
Markt —	market study
Urlaub (m)	
gestaffelter —	staggered holidays

V

variable Kosten (pl)	variable costs
variable Kostenrechnung (f)	variable costing
Varianz (f)	variance
— analyse (f)	variance analysis
Veralterung (f)	obsolescence
beabsichtigte —, geplante —	planned obsolescence
Verantwortlichkeit (f)	accountability, responsibility
funktionale — (en (pl))	functional responsibility
lineare —	linear responsibility

Zuteilung (*f*) der/von — en (*pl*) Verantwortung (*f*)	allocation of responsibilities
— sbezogene Erfassung (*f*) von Kosten (*pl*) und Leistungen (*fpl*)	responsibility accounting
lineare —	linear responsibility
Verarbeitung (*f*)	
Daten —	data processing
automatische —	automatic data processing (ADP)
elektronische —	electronic data processing (EDP)
Informations —	information processing
Stapel —	batch processing
Verband (*m*)	
Arbeitgeber — , Fach — , Wirtschafts —	trade association
Verbesserung (*f*)	
Gewinn —	profit improvement
Produkt —	product improvement
Verbindlichkeiten (*fpl*)	liabilities
kurzfristige — , laufende —	current liabilities
Verbraucher (*m*)	consumer, user
— einstellung (*f*)	user attitude
— erhebung (*f*)	user (attitude) survey
— forschung (*f*)	consumer research
— panel (*n*)	consumers' panel
— strategie (*f*)	user strategy
— verhalten (*n*)	consumer behaviour, user attitude
Anerkennung (*f*) als Markenartikel (*m*) durch den —	brand recognition
Produktablehnung (*f*) durch den —	consumer resistance
Produktannahme (*f*) durch den —	consumer acceptance
Verbrauchsgüter (*npl*)	consumer goods
Vereinbarung (*f*)	agreement
Produktivitäts —	productivity agreement
Lohnverhandlungen (*fpl*) mit — en (*pl*)	productivity bargaining
Arbeit (*f*) gemäss vertraglicher —	work by contract
Vereinfachung (*f*)	variety reduction
Arbeits —	work simplification
Stellen —	job simplification
Vereinigung (*f*)	amalgamation, merger

Verfahren (n)	procedure
— skontrolle (f)	process control
— zur Verwaltungskontrolle (f)	administrative control procedures
Aufteilungs — für Gemeinkosten (pl)	overheads recovery
— für indirekte Kosten (pl)	recovery of expenses
Beschwerde —	grievance procedure
Beurteilungs — nach Punkten	points rating method
Führungs — (pl)	management practices
administrative, verwaltungstechnische Kontroll — (pl)	administrative control procedures
Kostenaufteilungs —	absorption costing
Kostenspezifikations —	direct costing
Liquidations —	winding-up
logistisches —	logistic process
Schieds — , Schlichtungs —	arbitration
Systeme (npl) und — (pl)	systems and procedures
System —	systems approach
Vergleich (m)	
Betriebs —	interfirm comparison
Soll-/Ist- —	performance against objectives
Vergütung (f)	
— der Führungskräfte (fpl)	executive compensation
— neben Gehalt (n) oder Lohn (m)	fringe benefit
leistungsbezogene, leistungsgerechte, leistungsorientierte —	payment by results
Verhalten (n)	
— in der Organisation (f)	organisational behaviour
— sanalyse (f)	attitude survey
— sforschung (f)	behavioural science
Kauf —	buying behaviour
Verbraucher —	consumer behaviour, user attitude
Verhältnis (n)	
Arbeitgeber-Arbeitnehmer- —	labour relations
Deckungs —	cover ratio
Aktienpreis (m)/Ertrags —	price-earnings ratio (P/E)
Gewinn-/Umsatz —	profit-volume ratio (P/V)
Input-Output- — des Investitionsportefolios (n), Kapital-/Produktions —	capital-output ratio

Verhandlung (f)	
— sstrategie (f)	negotiation strategy
gemeinsame — (en (pl))	joint negotiation(s)
Lohn — en (pl) mit Produktivitätsvereinbarungen (fpl), Produktivitäts —	productivity bargaining
Tarif — en (pl)	collective bargaining
innerbetriebliche —	plant bargaining
Verkäufermarkt (m)	sellers' market
Verkauf (m)	
— sabteilung (f)	sales department
— sanalyse (f)	sales analysis
— sappell (m)	sales appeal
— sbudget (n)	sales budget
— serwartungen (fpl)	sales expectations
— sfördernd die verschiedenen — en Maßnahmen (fpl)	promotional mix
— sförderung (f)	
— smix, — spaket (n)	promotional mix
— spolitik (f)	promotional policy
— sgebiet (n)	sales area/territory
— sgespräch (n)	sales talk
— skampagne (f)	sales drive
— skontingent (n)	sales quota
— sleiter (m)	sales manager
— sleitung (f)	sales management, market management
— sort (m)	point of sale
— spolitik (f)	selling policy, promotion policy
aggressive —	hard selling
neutrale —	soft selling
— spotential (n)	sales potential
— sprogramm (n)	sales mix
— sschätzung (f)	sales estimate
Abdeckung (f) durch den —	sales coverage
aggressive — smethoden (fpl)	hard selling
Bemühungen (fpl) um — ssteigerungen (fpl)	sales expansion effort
Debitoren —	factoring
Direkt —	direct selling
Kundendienst (m) nach dem — Verlauf (m)	after-sales service
Konjunktur —	economic trend
verlustbringendes Produkt (n)	loss maker
Vermittlung (f) von Führungskräften (fpl)	executive search

Vermögen (*n*)	
— sbildung (*f*)	capital formation
— sertrag (*m*)	earnings on assets
Anlage —	fixed assets
Neubewertung (*f*) des — s	revaluation of assets
Funds —	asset value
Gesellschafts —	net worth
greifbare — swerte (*mpl*)	tangible assets
Netto —	net assets
Umlauf —	current assets
Netto — , Nettowert (*m*) des — s	net current assets
Verpackung (*f*)	packaging
Verrechnungspreise (*mpl*)	
Festlegung (*f*) der —	transfer pricing
Verschmelzung (*f*)	amalgamation
Verschuldungsgrad (*m*)	debt ratio
Versetzung (*f*) der Mitarbeiter (*mpl*)	staff transfer
verspätete Reaktion (*f*)	lag response
Versuchsproduktion (*f*)	pilot production
Verteilung (*f*)	
Häufigkeits —	frequency distribution
innerbetriebliche Waren —	physical distribution management
vertikale Integration (*f*)	vertical integration
Vertrag (*m*)	contract
Tarif —	collective bargaining agreement
vertraglich	
Arbeit (*f*) gemäß — er Vereinbarung (*f*)	work by contract
Vertreter (*m*)	
Allein —	sole agent
Vertretung (*f*)	
— der Arbeitnehmer (*mpl*)	worker representation
gemeinsame —	joint representation
Vertrieb (*m*)	
— skette (*f*)	chain of distribution
— skosten (*pl*)	distribution costs
— -und Gewinnaufschlag (*m*)	mark-up
— sleiter (*m*)	distribution manager
— snetz (*n*)	distribution network
— splanung (*f*)	distribution planning
— spolitik (*f*)	distribution policy
— swege (*mpl*)	channels of distribution
verwalten	to manage
Verwaltung (*f*)	administration

— der liquiden Mittel (*npl*)	cash management
— sgemeinkosten (*pl*)	administrative over-heads
— stheorie (*f*)	administrative theory
— von Kapitalanlagen (*fpl*)	investment management
Finanz —	financial administration, management
Kredit —	credit management
Portefeuille —	portefolio management
System —	systems management
Verfahren (*npl*) zur — skon-trolle (*f*), — stechnische Kontrollverfahren (*npl*)	administrative control procedures
Verwendbarkeit (*f*)	
vielseitige — der Mitarbeiter (*mpl*), vielseitige — des Personals (*n*)	staff mobility
Verzeichnis (*n*)	
Gehalts —	payroll
vielseitige Verwendbarkeit (*f*) der Mitarbeiter (*mpl*), des Personals (*n*)	staff mobility
Vize-Präsident (*m*)	vice president
Vollmacht (*f*)	
Linien —	line authority
Volumen (*n*)	volume
Kosten-/Gewinn-/ — analyse (*f*)	cost, volume, profit analysis
Umsatz —	sales volume
Voranschlag (*m*)	
Systemkosten —	estimating systems costs
Vorarbeiter (*m*)	foreman
Voraussage (*f*)	
Konjunktur —	business forecasting
Vorbereitungszeit (*f*)	lead time
Vorgabe (*f*)	
— leistung (*f*)	standard performance
Führung (*f*) durch — von Programmen (*npl*)	programmed manage-ment
Führung (*f*) durch — von Zielen (*npl*)	management by objectives (MBO)
Leistungs —	performance standards
vorgegebenes System (*n*) zur Messung (*f*) von Bewegung (*f*) und Zeit (*f*)	predetermined motion time system (PMTS)
Vorgehen (*n*)	
—der Unternehmensleitung (*f*)	top management approach

153

System — systems approach
Vorgesetzte(r) (*m*) supervisor
Vorschlagswesen (*n*) suggestion scheme
Vorschrift (*f*)
  Dienst (*m*) nach — work-to-rule
Vorsitzende(r) (*m*) chairman
  stellvertretender — deputy chairman, vice-chairman
  Vorstands — chief executive
vorsorgliche Instandhaltung, preventive maintenance
  vorsorgliche Wartung (*f*)
Vorsprung (*m*)
  Wettbewerbs — competitive edge
Vorstandsvorsitzende(r) (*m*) chief executive
Vorstoß (*m*)
  Wettbewerbs — competitive thrust
Vorteil (*m*)
  Wettbewerbs — competitive advantage
Vorwärtsplanung (*f*) forward planning

W

Wachstum (*n*)
  — sbereich (*m*), — sgebiet (*n*) growth area, expansion area
  — sindex (*m*) growth index
  — sindustrie (*f*) growth industry
  — spotential (*n*) growth potential
  — sstrategie (*f*) growth strategy, expansion strategy
  Unternehmens — corporate growth
Wahl (*f*)
  — der Werbemittel (*npl*) media selection
  — freier Zugriff (*m*) random access
  — zwischen Eigenfertigung (*f*) make-or-buy decision
  und Kauf (*m*)
Wahrscheinlichkeitstheorie (*f*) probability theory
Ware (*f*)
  — nsortiment (*n*) product mix
  innerbetriebliche — nverteil- physical distribution
  ung (*f*) management
  Halbfertig — (n) (*pl*) work-in-progress
Warteschlangentheorie (*f*) queueing theory
Wartung (*f*)
  geplante — planned maintenance
Wechsel (*m*)
  — beziehungen (*fpl*) interface
  strategische — strategic interdependence

— wirkung (*f*)	trade-off
Wege (*mpl*)	
Absatz —	channels of distribution
Festlegung (*f*) der Handels —	routing
Kommunikations —	channels of communication
Vertriebs —	channels of distribution
Weisungsstruktur (*f*)	authority structure
Weiterentwicklung (*f*)	
persönliche —	personal growth
Werbe —	
— botschaft (*f*)	advertising message
— budget (*n*)	advertising budget
— etat (*m*)	advertising budget
bewilligter —	advertising appropriation
— feldzug (*m*)	advertising drive
— fonds (*m*)	advertising budget
bewilligter —	advertising appropriation
— forschung (*f*)	advertising research
— kampagne (*f*)	advertising campaign
— leiter (*m*)	advertising manager
— mittel (*npl*)	advertising media
bewilligte —	advertising appropriation
verstärkter Einsatz (*m*) der —	advertising drive
Wahl (*f*) der —	media selection
— mittler (*m*)	advertising agent
— n um	to canvass
— thema (*n*)	advertising theme
— träger (*m*)	advertising media
— wirksamkeit (*f*)	advertising effectiveness
verstärkter — einsatz (*m*)	advertising drive
Werbung (*f*)	
(An-) — von Führungskräften (*fpl*)	executive search
Kunden — durch Sonderangebote (*npl*)	leader merchandising, switch selling
Postversand —	direct mail
Produkt —	product advertising
Unternehmens —	corporate advertising
unterschwellige —	subliminal advertising
Werksleiter (*m*)	plant manager, works manager
Werkstattprinzip (*n*)	
Betriebsanlage (*f*) nach —	process equipment layout

155

Wert (*m*)
— analyse (*f*)	value analysis (VA)
— konzept (*n*)	value concept
— technik (*f*)	value engineering
— verschlechterung (*f*) durch Grundstückbelastung (*f*)	dilution of equity
Altmaterial — , Ausschlachtungs —	break-up value
Buch —	book value
Erfahrungs —	yardstick
Firmen —	goodwill
gegenwärtiger Netto —	net present value (NPV)
greifbare Vermögens — e (*pl*)	tangible assets
immaterielle — e (*pl*)	intangible assets
Markt —	market value
materielle — e (*pl*)	tangible assets
Mehr —	value added, added value (VA)
— steuer (*f*)	value added tax (VAT)
Methode (*f*) des gegenwärtigen — es	present value method
Mittel —	mean
Modal —	mode
Netto — des Umlaufvermögens (*n*)	net current assets
Substanz —	asset value
Wiederbeschaffungs —	replacement cost
Zentral —	median

Wesen (*n*)
Betriebsrechnungs —	management accounting
innerbetriebliches Förder —	materials handling
Transport —	materials handling
Vorschlags —	suggestion scheme

Wettbewerb (*m*)
— sanreiz (*m*)	competitive stimulus
— sbeschränkungen, — seinschränkungen (*fpl*)	restrictive practices (legal)
— sposition (*f*), — sstellung (*f*)	competitive position
— sstrategie (*f*)	competitive strategy
— staktik (*f*)	competitive tactics
— svorsprung (*m*)	competitive edge
— svorstoß (*m*)	competitive thrust
— svorteil (*m*)	competitive advantage

Wiederaufbau (*m*) des Unternehmens (*n*)	company reconstruction
Wiederbeschaffungskosten (*pl*), — wert (*m*)	replacement cost

Wiedergewinnung (*f*) von Informationen (*fpl*)	information retrieval
wilder Streik (*m*)	wildcat strike
wirksame Unternehmens- führung (*f*)	effective management, managerial effectiveness
Wirksamkeit (*f*)	effectiveness
Kosten —	cost effectiveness
organisatorische —	organisational effective- ness
Werbe —	advertising effectiveness
Wirt (*m*)	
Betriebs —	business economist
Wirtschaft (*f*)	
— licher Auftrag (*m*)	economic mission
— liche Lebensdauer (*f*) eines Produkts (*n*)	product life
— liche Losgröße (*f*)	economic batch quan- tity, order quantity
— liche Produktionsmenge (*f*)	economic manufactur- ing quantity
— sforschung (*f*)	economic research
— sinformation (*f*)	economic intelligence
— sjahr (*n*)	fiscal year
— sleben (*n*)	economic life
— sprognose (*f*)	environmental fore- casting
— stendenzen (*fpl*)	economic trend
— sverband (*m*)	trade association
Betriebs —	business management
Betriebs — ler (*m*)	business economist
Material —	materials handling
Wissenschaft (*f*) (von) der Betriebsführung, der Betriebsleitung (*f*)	management science
wissenschaftlich	
— er Beirat (*m*)	brains trust
— e Betriebsführung (*f*)	scientific management
— es Management (*n*)	scientific management
— e Programmierung (*f*)	scientific programming

Z

Z-Diagramm (*n*)	Z-chart
Zeit (*f*)	
— norm (*f*)	standard time
— planung (*f*)	scheduling
— serie (*f*)	time series

— studie (*f*)	time study, work measurement
— - und Bewegungsstudie (*f*)	time and motion study, time and methods study
Amortisations —	payback period
Anlauf —	lead time
Auftragsbearbeitungs —	lead time
Ausfall —	down time
Echt —	real time
Liefer —	lead time
Normal —	standard time
Real —	real time
Standard —	standard time
unmittelbar geleistete Arbeits —	direct labour
Vorbereitungs —	lead time
vorgegebenes System (*n*) zur Messung (*f*) von Bewegung (*f*) und —	predetermined motion time system (PMTS)
zulässiger — raum (*m*), zulässige — spanne (*f*) für unterdurchschnittliche Leistung (*f*)	time span of discretion
Zentrale (*f*)	head office
Computer- — , Computer-Dienst —	computer services bureau
Zentralisierung (*f*)	centralisation
Zentrum (*n*)	
Gewinn —	profit centre
Rechen —	computer centre
Ziel (*n*)	target, objective
— findung (*f*)	goal seeking
— hierarchie (*f*)	hierarchy of goals
— setzung (*f*)	goal/target setting, objective (setting)
Führung (*f*) durch Vorgabe (*f*) von — en (*pl*)	management by objectives (MBO)
gesamte — e (*pl*) des Unternehmens (*n*)	overall company objectives
Gewinn —	profit target, profit goal
Produktions — e (*pl*)	production targets
Umsatz —	sales target, goal
Unternehmens —	company goal, company objective
Unternehmens — e (*pl*)	company objectives
gesamte —	overall company objectives